Life Mapping

ALSO BY BILL COHEN

The Perfect Moment (FICTION)

Life Mapping

A UNIQUE APPROACH
TO FINDING YOUR VISION
AND REACHING
YOUR POTENTIAL

BILL COHEN

EAGLE BROOK

William Morrow and Company, Inc.

NEW YORK

Published by Eagle Brook
An Imprint of William Morrow and Company, Inc.
1350 Avenue of the Americas
New York, N.Y. 10019

It is the policy of William Morrow and Company, Inc., and its im-
prints and affiliates, recognizing the importance of preserving what
has been written, to print the books we publish on acid-free paper,
and we exert our best efforts to that end.

Library of Congress Cataloging-in-Publication Data
Cohen, Bill, 1947–
Life mapping : a unique approach to finding your vision and reaching your
potential / Bill Cohen.—1st ed.
p.   cm.
Includes bibliographical references.
ISBN 0-688-15573-1 (pbk.)
1. Self-actualization (Psychology)   2. Success—Psychological aspects.
3. Vocational guidance—Psychological aspects   I. Title.
BF637.S4C65   1998
158.1—dc21   97-38812
CIP

Printed in the United States of America

FIRST EDITION

1 2 3 4 5 6 7 8 9 10

BOOK DESIGN BY CATHRYN S. AISON

www.williammorrow.com

To my mother, Ann Josephine Brajkovich Cohen, who passed away on February 28, 1996. She gave me a foundation of love and understanding.

To my wife, Gail Roberta Wheat Cohen, who has helped me find my spirit.

Acknowledgments

I WISH TO THANK my grandmother, Mary Brajkovich, for showing me unconditional love; my mother and father, Ann and Dave Cohen, for supporting me and giving me the freedom necessary for me to find myself; my children, Emily and Josh, for their understanding and help during the writing phase; my editor Joann Davis for having faith in my ability; my editor Michelle Shinseki, the most positive, supportive person I know; my friends and coworkers for their support and encouragement; the Woodside Priory School for allowing me to bring Life Mapping to the school; and finally, my wife, Gail, for being the perfect partner.

Contents

We live our lives as if we were involved in a series of disasters rather than in an orderly process to achieve the natural results we desire.
—Admiral Bidcoff

Life Mapping

THE GATHERING

Q<small>UIET</small>! Can you hear it? What calls your heart? Something deep inside is stirring. Will you listen? Will you understand? Will you act? If you are ready, you will!

You are an amazing creature! No one else has your unique traits, skills, abilities, and capacity for acquiring wisdom. With them you can do anything, but what will you do?

To put the question another way: What is the most important thing you will do in your lifetime? Some might answer: successfully raise children, have an enjoyable career, or find the cure for cancer. All good answers. But are they really the *most* important? Will they bring you happiness and peace of mind?

Mencius, a Chinese Confucian who lived during the same time as Aristotle, was once asked an interesting question by his disciple Kung-too: "All are equally men, but some are great men, and some are little men—how is this?"

Mencius replied, "Those who follow that part of themselves which is great are great men; those who follow that part of themselves which is little are little men. Let a man first stand fast in the supremacy of the nobler part of his constitution, and the inferior part will not be able to take it from him. It is simply this which makes the great man."[1] Thus, we must discover our nobler part, or as Carlyle said, "Let each become all that he was created capable of being."

Life Mapping is a process that helps us to reach our full potential. It helps us remove the conflicts that prevent us from

3

becoming the person we were created to be. Those conflicts exist because there are inconsistencies in what we believe, the way we think, and ultimately in our behavior. It is these conflicts that confuse us and keep us from becoming the person we want to become. When the conflicts are gone, we feel whole. It is a healing process that allows us to reach our nobler part. We learn who we are and how we fit into this world. It is a process that calls those seeking their nobler part. It is "The Gathering" of our nobler parts.

What Have We Lost?

Have you noticed that Americans have become angry? In the first half of the twentieth century, you could walk down the street and receive pleasant greetings from almost everyone. Advertisements featured smiling people. Early television was dominated by shows like *The Adventures of Ozzie and Harriet*. Ozzie always had a smile on his face, even when he was mischievous. Sometime during the period from the mid-1950s to the end of the 1960s, our mood changed. Was it the Vietnam War? Are we angry at ourselves for being in it or losing it? Are we angry that some of our heroes—among them, John F. Kennedy, Malcolm X, Robert Kennedy, and Dr. Martin Luther King, Jr.— were assassinated? Whatever the cause, notice the results. Start looking at advertising, listening to some of the hard-driving modern music, and observe the way people drive their cars, or the looks people give you when you walk down the street. As Hall of Famer Harmon Killebrew put it, "The thing I notice [with today's ballplayers] is that they don't seem to be having as much fun as we used to." Even our high-priced entertainers seem mad at the world. Many of them act out this feeling in the way they perform and conduct their lives. It is not a pretty picture. If we have to be tough to survive, that will be the image we project.

Madison Avenue calls it attitude! Is this how a civilized society should act? Why are we so angry? Why do we fly off the handle when things don't go our way? Isn't the average American better off now than during the 1930s? Maybe some people feel guilty because they have so much. Maybe our sincere desire to do a good job has diminished. Maybe we expect everyone else to be looking out for themselves, so that we must be tough and look out for ourselves. Could our anger be the result of a feeling that no one else cares about us? Are we alone? Isolationism at its worst.

David Myers, a professor of psychology at Hope College in Michigan, tells us about happiness that "external circumstances matter surprisingly little, whether you're wealthy or physically disabled matters so much less than you'd guess." He researched thousands of studies on happiness to determine who is happy and why. The results of his work are found in his book *The Pursuit of Happiness*. Happy people should exhibit happy behavior. The average American's behavior during the last half of this century does not suggest that we are happy. This is true even though we have more of the external trappings and generally better circumstances than those living in the first half of the century. Thus, works like *The Pursuit of Happiness* are needed to move us toward the answer to this dilemma: We must look within ourselves if we are to find happiness.

Where Is Our Vision?

America has lost its way. We no longer have a vision of our future; nor do we have the visionaries who can lead us to it. Things are moving so quickly, most of us do not take the time to look past the crisis we are currently facing. Survival so preoccupies us that we run from the beast that chases rather than toward the goal of future happiness that beckons us. If we are to find happiness, it will be the result of a vision that like a beacon leads us there. But who will create that vision?

People feel lost and dissatisfied with their lives. Mothers are juggling careers and families, students are graduating without a sense of a career path, and the baby boomers are turning fifty unable to see the meaning in their lives. The Life Mapping process is a tool that is desperately needed in America today. During the past twenty-five years, divorce rates have risen dramatically, adolescent violence has also increased drastically, corporate crime has become routine, and the number of people living in poverty continues to grow at a similar pace—and all of these trends are out of control. And that is only the tip of the iceberg, the part that we can see. How could we ever really know the misery and desperation that lies just below the surface. People have no safe place for their vision, except deep within their own hearts, the only place no one else can enter and destroy it.

Our Past and Our Future

Understanding who we are, who we are capable of becoming, and how we fit into this world will require us to step back and look at the bigger picture. We need to understand that we are dependent upon the delicate balances in nature. If one small element, such as oxygen, were taken out of the mix, it would mean the end of humanity.

We must also think long range and globally. What will the long-term results be, generations into the future, of the world we are creating? No longer can one country or one continent ignore the rest of the world when planning its future. International organizations must learn to work together for the common good of all humanity. That will happen when enough individuals around the world unite behind a common cause. Governments are slow to change. Usually, change occurs only after a majority of the population *demands* it. Are you going to be part of the population that demands change?

The history of humanity is filled with ideas. As you study these ideas, you begin to see a trend. Concern for the development of humanity was the theme that ran through the lives and teachings of Abraham, Moses, the authors of the Vedas, Lao-tzu, Buddha, Confucius, Socrates, Aristotle, Jesus, Saint Augustine,

Muhammad, Saint Thomas Aquinas, René Descartes, William Law, Benjamin Franklin, David Hume, Immanuel Kant, Thomas Paine, Joseph Smith, Ralph Waldo Emerson, Abraham Lincoln, Søren Kierkegaard, Henry David Thoreau, and Mahatma Gandhi. Don't let the long list overwhelm you. The point is that even though people's lives have improved as technology evolved, the development of the human race was still the primary focal point. Principles such as honesty, loyalty, humility, and respect were stressed and became the moral foundation of most societies. It was sometime in the early twentieth century that things began to change. Then, the pace of life began to quicken. People were suddenly forced to make more decisions in a single day than their parents had made in a month or their great-grandparents had made in a whole year.

The ideas that had grounded those past generations began to blur, as sound principles were no longer passed on from one generation to the next. Our newest generation is forced to deal with this ever quickening pace without the benefit of the principles that helped their ancestors make the tough choices that life forces upon us. The modern world focuses more on amassing possessions, looking better, being more efficient, appearing smarter, acquiring skills, or just plain winning, at any cost. Just win, baby! Just do it! The more we emphasize winning, the more losers we create. Losers who need to figure out a way to win, *next time*. The results of the wave created by this kind of thinking are devastating.

I believe that this wave also leads us away from our nobler part. As we begin to do whatever it takes to win, we find that we have deviated from the inner blueprint that guides us to our nobler part. That inner blueprint has been given many names; consciousness, intuition, soul, spirit, karma, aura, or Tao. This deviation creates a conflict. We no longer see ourselves as the noble person we had hoped to become. The wave begins to build as our subconscious mind leads us to select new methods that support our new image of ourselves. Each day we move farther away from the person we are destined to become. Each day we are less happy with the person we are becoming. We can no longer allow ourselves the time to think about the conflict . . . it is now too painful. We are afraid to be alone with our thoughts, so we listen to music, watch television, immerse ourselves in work or play, sometimes all at once, anything to keep our minds busy.

Will this work? I don't think so. Our subconscious minds are still able to feel the conflict and we remain disturbed. Only now, we aren't sure why. We have the big house, the fancy car, and the great job. But we aren't satisfied. So we start looking for answers in all the wrong places. We get a divorce, change companies, yell at the kids, start drinking or smoking or snorting. When all the time the answer lay locked within us. If only we will stop the noise and commotion long enough to look inside for the answer. I believe that Samuel Johnson, the eighteenth-century English writer and lexicographer, referred to this problem when he wrote, "The fountain of content must spring up in the mind, and he who hath so little knowledge of human nature as to seek happiness by changing anything but his own disposition, will waste his life in fruitless efforts and multiply the grief he proposes to remove." Ask yourself this question: Am I becoming the person I really want to become? If not, do something about it, *now!*

This is where Life Mapping comes into play. It takes us from where we are to where we want to be. It is a process that helps us put our lives into perspective. It takes us through the steps necessary for us to find the answers that lie within us. Life Mapping helps us stop the noise and see beyond the superficial world of today, to a life of substance with deeper, clearer values. We create a vision of the people we really are destined to become. That vision will lead us to change the daily activities that define our lives. If we have been trustworthy in every activity involving our neighbors, our actions have defined us as trustworthy people. Once our activities are in alignment with our inner blueprint, we begin to live a life that we can define as successful.

You might be wondering what our inner blueprint is. It is the private, unique internal plan for our lives. It doesn't change, but our understanding of it does. The more we learn to listen and understand it, the closer we will be to living it and experiencing the joy associated with that alignment.

Life Mapping led my family from a world of money, possessions, and power to one of love and fellowship. The journey has not been an easy one and it is not completed. But the benefits far outweigh the effort required.

Seventeen years ago I was a manager with one of the largest insurance companies in the world. I used the basic Life Mapping techniques with all of the people I was managing. This group of individuals rose from 50th to 1st in sales and service in our region and from 1,150th to 38th in the company over a nine-year period. This was accomplished in a manner consistent with the integrity that grew out of the core beliefs and principles of the group. We resisted the pressure to shortcut our principles in order to receive instant recognition, preferring instead to hold fast to the belief that our devotion to correct principles would prove successful in the long run. Although we were always near the bottom of month-long promotion lists, by the end of the year we were always near the top of the lists. Our constant dedication to predetermined activities produced the desired results over the long run. Those routine activities may seem less than spectacular in the short run, but they have a compounding effect that produces extraordinary outcomes.

The inevitable result of the Life Mapping process is evolution. This evolution began to change the way I related to life in general. For example, the ambition for financial success began to take a backseat to the desire to become a more fully human person. The result has been a more peaceful, contented life. The wonders of nature have now become more evident to me. I no longer have the need to constantly acquire things; sharing has replaced that passion. My relationships with my seventeen-year-old son, Josh, my fifteen-year-old daughter, Emily, and most important, Gail, my wife, are wonderful and grounded in love. Life Mapping is the tool that has opened the lines of communication and led me to these rewarding and fulfilling relationships.

Ultimately, however, even the most successful life comes to

an end. Living a life that can be defined as successful also means enjoying the journey, as well as having few regrets when the journey ends. Which reminds me of the story of Alfred Bernhard Nobel (1833–1896), the founder of the Nobel Prize. He was a Swedish chemist and engineer, who in 1866 invented dynamite and made a fortune selling the formula. When his brother died, one newspaper ran Alfred's obituary by mistake, and when Alfred read the obituary he was shocked to see how he would be remembered, as the inventor of a means of mass destruction. He did not want to be remembered in that way, so he bequeathed his fortune to a foundation that would establish the Nobel Prize. What will be your legacy? I would like to think of you as the person you are capable of becoming, rather than anything less.

Choices

We can take the world as it comes to us and conform to that reality or we can identify our dreams, work to bring them to fruition, and in so doing help change the world into a better place for all humanity. Each of us sees the world through the filter of our own life. That means that reality is the sum of all our individual experience. Reality is one large puzzle and each of us is but one piece. But the puzzle is not complete without all the pieces. This is why every person is important in the final analysis. The English poet John Donne wrote, "No man is an island entire of itself; every man is a piece of the Continent, a part of the main. . . . Any man's death diminishes me because I am involved in Mankind; and therefore never send to know for whom the bell tolls; it tolls for thee."

Your foot is a part of you, just as you are part of humanity. We will not be complete until all of humanity is whole. We should work to eliminate the waste of human life that is so common today by finding our destiny and helping others do the same. Let us not squander Donne's insight. As another, anonymous, philosopher, has put it, "Like the shadow of a tree, our influence often falls where we are not."

So we can see that we are not only part of the whole of nature, but are also one piece of the puzzle of humanity. Not only must we learn to live in harmony with these realities, but we need to work to protect and nurture them. We must each seek opportunities to unite humanity and resolve situations that are divisive.

Now that we have seen the bigger picture and humanity's purpose, it is time to look at our individual purpose.

Charting Your Course

Visualize your life as a trip into some unknown country, where every turn has three or four forks in the road. When you are born, you are given an inner blueprint or map you are to follow. That blueprint determines the place you start your journey, like the city where you are born. If nothing else influences you, you will follow the predetermined route and know which fork to take, every time. As you take your first few steps, you begin to feel the influence of your environment. The people, places, and things you encounter begin to affect your decisions. The possible routes or lives you could live become unlimited. Each fork provides a whole new series of possibilities. Now comes the difficult part. Some of those lives are filled with happiness and fulfillment, while others bring only misery and regrets. How are we to know which forks to take?

We can attack this problem from two basic points of view. We can accept life as it comes to us and deal with the forks as they appear or we can develop instruments that will lead us toward one of the lives that brings us the desired outcomes. Most people take the first option. They live not by choice, but by default. As Admiral Bidcoff, the man responsible for coordinating emergency services for the city of San Francisco, puts it, "We live our lives as if we were involved in a series of disasters rather than in an orderly process to achieve the natural results we desire." Some might escape this destiny and still be happy. But most will endure a life filled with regrets. Others will find

that a small decision made years before has forced them onto a
route with no possible chance for happiness. This is what Life
Mapping is all about: taking the inner blueprint we were born
with and using it to create an extraordinary life, the one we deserve. What your life is now isn't as important as what your life
will become. See your future and live it.

Where Do Our Choices Lead Us?

The American psychologist Abraham Maslow once said,
"A musician must make music, an artist must paint, a poet must
write, if he is to be ultimately at peace with himself."[2] Being in
alignment with our inner blueprint brings the peace of which
Maslow speaks. That is why so many people think of their lives
as meaningless. Without the satisfaction that living in alignment
with our inner blueprint brings, we experience boredom, angst,
and unhappiness. When we achieve this alignment, we stop running to some unknown destination. Our purpose summons us
instead to make music or paint or write or use whatever gifts
we were given. The world is waiting for our gifts.

It is easy to be fooled into thinking that having fun is our
chief aim in life. When we are wealthy enough, we can have fun
all day long! But fun without *purpose* soon loses its allure. How
many famous people have killed themselves because fun just
wasn't enough? Fun is what makes the journey enjoyable, but
the journey must have a worthwhile objective for it to have any
real meaning for most of us. When we understand what our true
purpose is and start living that journey, we will not need to
worry about having fun along the way.

Steve Martin's character in *Leap of Faith* is a fake preacher/
healer. He takes his fancy show on the road, bilking the bump-
kins in towns all over America. He is having fun, but seems
somehow unfulfilled. Then one day a miracle happens. He cures
a crippled boy and brings rain to a drought-ridden town. He is
so surprised and moved by the experience that he decides to
leave everything and everybody. During the last few hours lead-

ing up to his hitching a ride out of town in a truck, you feel him changing as he realizes that he had not been fulfilling his destiny. As he sits in the cab of the truck, you see the pure joy and freedom he experiences as he begins to live his life in alignment with his inner blueprint. He is off to create the life he was destined to live. How will you feel when you begin living the life you were destined to live? Remember, the world is waiting for your gift!

We all need help finding our gifts. Will a completed Life Map help us find our gifts? Can you imagine heading off to visit your best friend at her new home, without directions? The right map would be indispensable. The map would provide you with a variety of routes from which to choose. You might pick the most direct route or the most scenic for your journey. The odds of reaching your friend's home, and enjoying the trip, would be substantially increased. A Life Map is a map of your life with your basic route identified. There will be changes along the way but having the Life Map will give you a much better chance of success in life.

In 1953, Yale University graduates were interviewed to determine who had written goals and devised plans for achieving them. In 1973, this same group was interviewed again, this time to determine whether those who had written down their goals had really become more successful. The 3 percent who had done so in 1953 had achieved more professional success than the other 97 percent combined. They also seemed happier and better adjusted. Remember, they all had graduated from Yale University! Yes, written plans do work! Yes, a completed and followed Life Map will work!

We all want to become successful. Most of us were born with that trait. One of the problems we have in achieving good results is defining success for ourselves. A Life Map will help us define our meaning of success. It will unlock the inner resources that are within us. A Life Map is our personal plan for reaching our unique destiny. The Life Mapping process will take you through the steps necessary to determine what really matters to you. Incredibly, most of us spend most of our lives doing things we really don't want to do. That is true of every aspect of our lives. This world is moving so quickly that we continue to let circumstances or other people decide our everyday activities for us. Those are the very activities that define our lives. We seem to find the whole thing too difficult to deal with, and so we watch our lives as if we were watching a play, unable to control or change anything that happens in it. Thoreau aptly described this situation when he wrote, "The mass of men lead lives of quiet desperation." Don't be one of those people. Take the time to think about your life and to create a life that you will love. Shift directions now and create a new life from the inside out. Don't be one of those lost souls who looks back on their life and says, "This was not the life I was supposed to live!"

Great achievements and lives are built on a solid foundation of dreams. They are created in the mind first, on paper second, and finally in the daily activities that lead to their accomplishment. Wise people take their dreams of the world and their tomorrows, and begin living them immediately. You can't wait for a perfect situation before you change. You must first change your daily activities, and then the world and your tomorrows will follow. Which is more difficult: to stop what you are doing, develop a Life Map of your future and begin living it today, or to accept life as it is with the pain and regrets that will surely follow for the majority of us? They are two very different paths. On which path does a person truly suffer more? May you take the advice of Robin Williams's character in the movie *Dead Poets Society* when he tells his students to make their lives extraordinary, to gather their rosebuds while they may and to seize the day. *Carpe diem!*

Imagination

Your Life Map begins with an exploration of your imagination. Instead of discovering new worlds, you discover *your* world. You learn to define yourself and your role in that world. This part of the process requires you to understand your own belief system and the list of principles you believe you should follow. Why is this important? Most of us would describe ourselves as truthful. When we lie to others, we define ourselves as liars. Our conscious mind may hold on to the false opinion that we are truthful, but our subconscious mind discerns the deception. We have created a conflict. That conflict works to destroy the foundation our life is built upon. We think less of ourselves, and our subconscious mind begins to sabotage us. If we make a habit of lying, we begin to find lying less and less painful, until one day even our conscious mind concedes and we begin to rationalize that it's acceptable because everybody lies. It was the action in direct conflict with our belief that began this negative spiral. Keeping our actions in alignment with our beliefs is at the heart of the Life Mapping process. What are the steps?

- Learn to remove the conflicts in your life. You begin by *understanding your own belief system.*
- *Develop your list of principles,* each supported by one, or more, of your own beliefs.
- *Establish goals* in every area of your life, making sure that those goals do not create a conflict with any of your beliefs or principles.
- *Create a list of activities* for each goal. These are the activities that are required for you to achieve your goal.
- Finally, *develop an ideal weekly schedule,* which includes all of the activities.

Now, not only will your actions lead you to your goals, but they will define *you* as the person you really believe you are. As you live your Life Map, your vision of the future will begin to clarify. If you have been walking in a dense fog, your vision will become clearer and you will see the changes you need to make to improve your Life Map and your future. You will continue to update your Life Map as you proceed. It is a *process,* not a goal. One day you will look back in wonder at how far you have come. Your Life Map and the vision that results will sustain you through all of life's challenges. You will be ready for them! You will thrive in spite of them!

The Life Mapping Process

Life Mapping is a five-step process.

1. Determining your *beliefs*
2. Developing your *principles*
3. Deciding on your *goals*
4. Dividing the goals into the necessary *activities*
5. Designing your *schedule* of activities

Beliefs form the fabric you use to make your map. Without good, solid material your map will wear out before you reach your destination. Principles are the rules or laws of the roads you will travel, on the way to reaching your destination. Goals are your chosen destinations, places worthy of your efforts. Activities are the roads that you will travel to reach those destinations. Once you have chosen your destination (your goal), you can decide which roads (activities) will help you reach them. A schedule is the itinerary you will use to make sure you know where you are supposed to be each day.

Goals help you decide which road to take (which choice to make) when you reach forks in the road (choices in life). You begin to make better and better decisions. You clearly see the progress in your journey. This leads to increased confidence and makes future decisions easier to make. As you develop your Map, you should occasionally check to make sure that you are not creating conflicts with your inner blueprint. Those conflicts, if studied, uncover the true motives behind your activities. Staying true to your inner blueprint keeps you from being led by wants created by others. Others will attempt to influence you through peer pressure and advertising, hoping to make you put their wants above your own true needs. Henry David Thoreau thought that the problem with Americans was that they have turned themselves into "mere machines" to acquire wealth without asking why. Thoreau bore the uncomfortable truth that material and moral progress were not as intimately related as Americans liked to think. He expressed these thoughts in the 1840s after spending considerable time away from civilization. What would he think of America in the 1990s?

Finding Our Path

I don't want to change you into my vision of you. Rather, I want to motivate you into becoming the person you are capable of becoming. It may seem hard at first, but soon the activities that you determine to be correct for you will become habits and it will be easier to stay on your new path than to go back to the old. According to Thoreau:

> I learned this, at least, by my experiment; that if one advances confidently in the direction of his dreams, and endeavors to live the life which he has imagined, he will meet with a success unexpected in common hours. Why should we be in such desperate haste to succeed, and in such desperate enterprises? . . . If a man does not keep pace with his companions, perhaps it is because he hears a different drummer. Let him step to the music which he hears, however measured or far away. [*Walden*]

Thoreau wants us to understand that living the life you imagine might be different from the life other people have expected. Have the courage to take your time, to find your path, and success will follow. Life Mapping as defined by Henry David Thoreau!

Character Counts

Dr. Laura Schlessinger, the popular talk-show host, in *How Could You Do That?! The Abdication of Character, Courage, and Conscience*, stresses that today's "victim" mentality has become an excuse for not accepting personal responsibility. The excuse goes something like this: "Considering my hurts, disappointments, and traumas, I can't be responsible for the havoc I wreak in the lives of others or the mess I've made of my own life." Dr. Schlessinger asks if anyone really believes this rationalization. If this were true, only people with exceptional genes, great parents, and an ideal environment could live lives of character, courage, and conscience. Everyone else would be doomed to some degree of failure. The victim mentality we have fostered steals the very hope, from those who need it most, that they can and will respond to whatever crisis has befallen them.

Keith, twenty-one, was addicted to drugs for eight years. "I took anything," he admitted, "to have fun with my friends. It was a blast. I just liked it." Now he is free from the drugs. "I had some long-range goals, and they just weren't panning out," Keith told Dr. Schlessinger. "I tried changing jobs, friends, love relationships, and still wasn't getting anywhere. Then I realized that I was the constant in the equation, and the constant was that I was using drugs."

Keith wasn't diseased. He wasn't a victim. He just made bad choices. Victim mentality blurred the lines between right and wrong. A vicious game of two wrongs make a right begins to escalate into chaos. Dr. Schlessinger sums it up, "After listening to people's stories for almost two decades, I have concluded that the path to healthy relationships and self-respect starts with the decision to do the right thing." That is what Life Mapping is all about, helping you decide what is the right thing and giving you a system within which to do it.

Most people have waited their whole lives for someone to come along and save them. They will be saved only when they realize that the person they have waited for is none other than themselves! If you have found it difficult to overcome your weaknesses, it is because the freedom you seek has not been preceded by the proper vision of that freedom. Create your vision! Create your Map! As the famous nineteenth-century writer George Eliot said, "It is never too late to be what you might have been."

Beliefs

According to William James: "Man alone, of all the creatures of earth, can change his own pattern. Man alone is architect of his destiny. The great revolution in our generation is the discovery that human beings, by changing the inner attitudes of their minds can change the outer aspects of their lives."[1]

How do we change the inner attitudes of our minds? Our attitudes are shaped by that which we truly believe. Without a clear idea of what we truly believe, we are like animals, and our attitudes are shaped by our environment. We abdicate control of our attitudes and thereby our lives to anyone willing to take the time to influence us. Once this is understood, we can reshape our attitudes by clearly defining what we truly believe. The act of writing down our beliefs is the first step in gaining control of our lives.

Beliefs drive every human behavior. What do you believe? If you have a well-defined Belief List, and act upon it, you should be happy with your behavior, most of the time. Without a well-defined Belief List, you will find yourself living someone else's life. The behavior associated with that life will reflect the combined influences of the many people trying to run your life for you, including those companies willing to spend billions of dollars to influence your behavior through advertising. Remember, in the final analysis, it is our behavior that defines us.

Our beliefs form the fabric we use to make our Life Map. Without good, solid material our map will wear out before we reach our destination. Our Belief List must include the understanding that we can become the person we see in our vision. It is our opportunity to experience our innermost being. We must be able to see ourselves fulfilling our purpose. What is our purpose? Purpose—the reason one exists. *The reason one exists!* That is a rather sobering thought. Can you really have a purpose? You can, you do, and you wouldn't be here if you didn't. Neither counselors, psychologists, or parents, nor priests, ministers, or rabbis are able to tell you your purpose. You need to discover it. You will find it deep within you. Not everyone has the same purpose. You are the only one who knows your true inner feelings, the things that bring you joy. Notice that I said joy, not pleasure. Pleasure can be a momentary thing, while joy is lasting. You feel that joy when you align your activities with your purpose or blueprint. You might think that some of the things that bring you joy are trivial, but nothing is trivial if it brings you and/or others joy. Something as simple as telling stories to children might be your purpose. That might be the very reason you are here. You could be the storyteller who brings a child's dreams to life.

My mother had a purpose; it was to make others feel comfortable. She didn't get paid to do this. She just did it every day, every time she saw you. Many strangers became her friend and she brightened their day and lightened their load whenever they saw her. You could see the joy in her face the moment she began a conversation with a newfound friend. It was as if the rest of the world had disappeared, as she and her new friend shared a piece of themselves. Some people confuse purpose with career. Your purpose might be somehow connected to your career. Or, as with my mother, it might be a gift you are here to give to others.

There are two parts to the purpose question: finding your individual purpose and finding the purpose of humanity in general. This world is very complex and interdependent. Given enough time and resources, you could eventually discover the purpose of every plant and animal. As noble an activity as that might seem, it would still be slightly less important than discovering your own purpose. How would knowing your purpose change the way you lived your life? Most people would live radically different lives if they knew why they were here. Unfortunately, they receive no training and have very little time to explore the concept. It might even seem like an impossible task. However, it is less complicated than you might imagine. It all begins with your idea of how and why we are here and the study of your individual gifts.

Finding Your Passion

Gifts are those skills you have that allow you to do some things better than most other people. For example, the talent behind the way Michael Jordan plays basketball, Tiger Woods plays golf, or Bill Gates runs Microsoft. You might have always thought that you were without any such special gift. But think again, because everyone has some. Try asking your friends, your spouse, or your siblings about your gifts. Think about the things you enjoy doing. You might have to extract the common elements from several different activities before the picture becomes clear enough for you to see. When you find your gifts, they will lead you to your purpose.

My mother had the gift of easy conversation with strangers. She developed friends from strangers within minutes. Many of those strangers became lifelong friends. My mother died last year and one of those friends now writes to me, since she no longer has my mother to share herself with. They used to be neighbors but for the past twenty years a thousand miles had separated them and they were only able to see each other a few times. But she never forgot my mother. They kept in touch by telephone and letters over the years.

Looking for Our Gifts

Children bring a wonderful sense of adventure and awe to the world. Time and adults slowly drain these gifts from all but the few lucky enough to escape childhood with them still intact.

Adam Werbach wrote an article titled "Three Little Words" for the *Sierra Club Bulletin* in which he tells of a group of researchers who asked a preschool class, "Who knows how to sing?" Every child eagerly responded that they could. "Who knows how to dance?" Same response. "Who knows how to draw?" You guessed it; every child responded positively. The following week, the researchers were asking the same questions of the students of an elite university. "Who knows how to sing?" A few responded that they could sing. "Dance?" Two reluctantly responded yes. "Draw?" Not one hand.

It seems that somewhere between preschool and college we lose these abilities. How do we lose them? Are we letting society slowly drain them from us with each negative response to our own individual expression of who we are. Are our children losing their abilities, or are they losing their confidence in their abilities? Those abilities are but a small sampling of the gifts that are taken from us as we "grow up," whatever that means. A child's world is full of wonder and excitement. If we could but nurture that feeling, it would serve as an antidote for the ills of boredom and disenchantment waiting along life's path. We must each work to reacquire these gifts and to make sure that our children never lose them. It is a gentle world that these gifts allow us to see, a world full of hope and optimism in which all problems can be overcome. That is the truth to which we are born. We can't let the harsh realities of this world spoil our chances to find a better one.

Look for your gifts to lead you to your purpose. I was born to be a teacher. It has taken me fifty years to figure that out. My early training was all centered around making as much money as possible. I was taught who makes the most and why. So when it came time for me to find a career, long-term financial success was the most important element. How could I make the most money? I decided that some form of sales would provide the best financial potential. I worked as a stockbroker for three years, from 1972 to 1975. Unfortunately, the timing was bad. I watched the Dow Jones Average fall from 1,060 to 560 the last twenty-four months of my career. I looked for another career, one that would provide a more stable income, and found the insurance business. Now, looking back, I can clearly see that I enjoyed teaching people new things. I was always teaching someone how to bowl, play bridge, or write a difficult computer program. Seeing people understand a new concept or solve a difficult problem has always provided me with a sense of pure joy! I guess that is why "joy" is at the center of the word "enjoyed." What brings you joy?

It Is a Matter of Perspective

"What you see and hear depends a good deal on where you are standing; it also depends on what sort of person you are," reads a line from C. S. Lewis's *The Magician's Nephew*.[2] This Lewis quote reminds me of a story. A man was sitting on a fence at the edge of a small western town in the late nineteenth century. A family in a wagon stopped to ask the man what kind of people lived in the town. The man asked about the kind of people the family experienced in their last town. The family replied that they left because most of the people were mean and cruel. The man responded by informing them that they would find the same kind of people in this town. A few hours later another family came along asking the same question. This time the family informed the man that the people in their last town were mostly kind and gentle. The man told them that they would find the same kind of people in this town. Now, it might seem at first glance that the man was just appeasing these people. A deeper look will reveal that the man was demonstrating one of the most solid principles of human interaction.

We as humans will find what we are looking for. If we look for the good in people, we will find it, and if we look for the bad in people, we will find it. The same people can often be seen from almost totally opposite points of view. This is the very point that Lewis makes. If we are to change the world we live in and the way people respond to us, we need to change the way we look at situations; we need to change our attitudes. Life Mapping is a tool that will help us, and the first step, the one

that determines where we are standing, is developing our Belief
List. Everything else is built on this foundation.

According to James Allen:

> What we are was designed and built by our own thoughts
> in our minds. If we nurture ignorant or evil thoughts, pain
> will soon follow. If our thoughts are healthy and benefi-
> cial, joy will follow us as surely as our shadows follow us
> on a sunny day. . . . Most of us are anxious to improve
> our circumstances, but are unwilling to improve our-
> selves—and we therefore remain bound. If we do not
> shrink from the honest self-examination we can never fail
> to accomplish the object upon which our hearts are set. . . .
> Law, not confusion, is the dominating principle in the uni-
> verse; justice, not injustice, is the soul and substance of life;
> and righteousness, not corruption, is the molding and
> moving force in the spiritual government of the world.
> This being so, we have to but right ourselves to find that
> the universe is right; and during the process of putting
> ourselves right, we will find that as we alter our thoughts
> towards things and other people, things and other people
> will alter towards us. [*As a Man Thinketh*][3]

Guard your thoughts, keep them as pure as you can, and they
will serve you well.

How Did It All Begin?

I would like you to begin your Belief List by asking that
most basic of all questions: How did it all begin? What do you
believe? Could it be the result of chaos leading to evolution, the
work of God, some combination of the two, or some other totally
different idea? In 1994 a Gallup poll found that 96 percent of
Americans believe in God. Of course, they have different de-
scriptions and names for God. Some think that God is somehow
responsible for evolution. Current scientific evidence has con-

fused the average person. That confusion has led people to abandon the question, in favor of faith or disbelief.

The issue here is for you to resolve the question to your own satisfaction. You can listen to the arguments on both sides, but in the final analysis, you must decide.

Life's Purpose

Your concept of how life began will help you to formulate your conception of the purpose of life in general and eventually—with the knowledge of your particular gifts, those that bring you true joy—of your individual purpose. How will this knowledge help you understand your purpose? An example might help answer this question. Perhaps you believe we were all put on this earth by God and that we have a collective purpose. You could further assume that the sum of our individual purposes will lead to the collective purpose. It would follow then that God would give each of us unique skills and abilities that would enable us to accomplish our individual purpose. So to find our individual purpose, we would only need to study ourselves to determine our unique skills and abilities. I have found teaching to be one of my special gifts. What special gifts have you been given? We can't wait for someone to come along and tell us how it all began or what is our individual purpose. We need to seek the answers ourselves. Whether God is in your idea of creation or not, you can create a Belief List. Armed with this list of your beliefs about the creation, you will be able to develop your Belief List. The answers to these questions lie within each of us. The struggle comes from the freeing of this information. Here is an exercise to help get you started.

On an individual sheet of paper, or in a journal or notebook, take some time to record your concept of the purpose of life in general.

_____

_____

After you have done this, write a statement in which you describe your individual purpose.

_____

_____

Here is a good working definition of a belief: "the mental acceptance of and conviction in something believed to be true." If you have the conviction and accept something to be true, it should be included in your list. Every time you add a new belief, ask yourself why you believe it. Your answer will lead you to deeper, more basic beliefs. The idea behind making a Belief List is to create a list that summarizes your major beliefs. There is no correct number of beliefs. However, if a stranger read your list, they would have a good sense of your idea of how it all began, the purpose of humanity in general, and your purpose specifically. There is a Suggested Reading list at the end of this book that might help you with this activity. Be patient with yourself; there is no reason to be in a hurry to create your list. Read, visit with people who might already have a well-defined Belief List, and take the time to think about all of the options. Most important, listen to that little voice in your head. It is your inner blueprint speaking to you.

Here is a sample of a quality Belief List, written by John D. Rockefeller, Jr. (1874–1960):

- *I believe* in the supreme worth of the individual and in his right to life, liberty, and pursuit of happiness.
- *I believe* that every right implies a responsibility; every opportunity, an obligation; every possession, a duty.
- *I believe* that the law was made for man and not man for the law; that government is the servant of the people and not their master.
- *I believe* in the dignity of labor, whether with head or hand; that the world owes no man a living, but that it owes every man an opportunity to make a living.
- *I believe* that thrift is essential to well-ordered living and that economy is a prime requisite of a sound financial

structure, whether in government, business, or personal affairs.

- *I believe* that truth and justice are fundamental to an enduring social order.
- *I believe* in the sacredness of a promise, that a man's word should be as good as his bond; that character—not wealth or power or position—is of supreme worth.
- *I believe* in an all-wise and all-loving God, named by whatever name, and that the individual's highest fulfillment, greatest happiness, and widest usefulness are to be found in living in harmony with His will.
- *I believe* that love is the greatest thing in the world; that it alone can overcome hate; that right can and will triumph over might.[4]

Please note that Rockefeller stated his beliefs in a very positive manner. There is no room for doubt in a belief. It is helpful to begin each belief with the words, *"I believe."* Until we understand our origin and our purpose, and develop a clear Belief List, we will be at the mercy of those who would influence us for their own benefit. Take control of your life, develop your Belief List, now! Here is a list of sample beliefs taken from those submitted by students in my Life Mapping classes. It might give you some ideas as you create your own Belief List.

Sample Beliefs

1. I believe people should not live alone; associating and communicating with others is essential.
2. I believe a sense of humor can be one's greatest asset.
3. I believe all people are interconnected and therefore their decisions affect other people.
4. I believe all people deserve respect.

5. I believe all people have the capacity to love and accept others.
6. I believe all people have the right to speak their mind.
7. I believe all people possess the capacity to do good.
8. I believe beauty is relative.
9. I believe challenging oneself to higher, more difficult levels is the path to finding yourself.
10. I believe education leads to better decisions.
11. I believe every being is unique.
12. I believe every cruel act is punished.
13. I believe every person needs to be loved . . . and needs to know it.
14. I believe every problem has a solution.
15. I believe everyone can be honest.
16. I believe everyone can find some happiness in their lives, no matter what the situation.
17. I believe everyone makes mistakes.
18. I believe everyone wants to be happy.
19. I believe everyone wants to be loved and valued.
20. I believe everything and everyone has a purpose.
21. I believe there is a reason for everything.
22. I believe everyone has the right to express their uniqueness.
23. I believe in forgiving others.
24. I believe freedom should be limited only by what is harmful to others, in the other's mind.
25. I believe in God.
26. I believe in the Golden Rule.
27. I believe government should protect the righteous and punish those who abuse the law.

28. I believe helping others leads to love instead of hate.
29. I believe honesty is necessary to have a genuine relationship.
30. I believe if people thought before they acted there would be fewer problems.
31. I believe ignorance and inflexibility are at the core of all catastrophes.
32. I believe ignorance prevents people from becoming happy.
33. I believe there is a degree of learning in all suffering.
34. I believe in compromise.
35. I believe that the Lord has given each of us free agency to choose right from wrong, and from these experiences we form our character.
36. I believe in evolution.
37. I believe in failure; without it you will never succeed.
38. I believe in family.
39. I believe in freedom for all.
40. I believe in God and His power to change the world through our prayers.
41. I believe that I am in control of my mind, thoughts, and actions; and the only thing I can't control are natural occurrences, and other people because they have also been given free agency.
42. I believe in life after death.
43. I believe in love.
44. I believe in miracles.
45. I believe in myself.
46. I believe in order to love someone else, you must first know and love yourself.
47. I believe in sharing.
48. I believe we all have God-given talents that need to be found, strengthened, and shared with other human beings.

49. I believe in the fundamental goodness of all life.
50. I believe in the importance of families and
      how they contribute to society.
51. I believe insecurity prevents us from doing
      what we believe we should.
52. I believe it is never too late to do something
      new or try again.
53. I believe in justice for all.
54. I believe lies only breed more lies.
55. I believe in life and that its uniqueness
      should be respected.
56. I believe life is sacred.
57. I believe life is short, and one must enjoy it.
58. I believe life should be balanced.
59. I believe no one has the right to judge others
      or impose their beliefs upon them.
60. I believe no one is perfect.
61. I believe no one should give in to peer pressure.
62. I believe nobody should be prejudged.
63. I believe one must not blame others but
      realize one's own mistakes.
64. I believe only ignorance prevents people from
      reaching their goals and finding their
      purpose.
65. I believe life is a journey of self-discovery.
66. I believe people are responsible for their lives.
67. I believe people desire to become fully human.
68. I believe people have the ability to change
      their lives.
69. I believe people should be true to themselves.
70. I believe people should not be criticized for
      their looks, dress, etc.; they are expressions
      of their individuality.
71. I believe people should not be selfish or greedy.
72. I believe people should think of the
      consequences of an action before they act.
73. I believe that we are here to contribute
      something.

74. I believe personal pain is never an excuse to cause others pain.
75. I believe physical beauty, though pleasing to the eye, is worthless without emotion.
76. I believe possessions are not as important as people think they are.
77. I believe privileges and responsibility go hand in hand.
78. I believe responsibility follows every action; one must be able to recognize mistakes and learn from them.
79. I believe self-expression should not interfere with the rights of others.
80. I believe, sometimes, your best friend is yourself.
81. I believe one of my purposes is to communicate love to my family as an example of God's love.
82. I believe that going against one's beliefs hurts oneself more than anyone else.
83. I believe that I should take control of my life.
84. I believe in the big bang theory.
85. I believe the happiest moment is the accomplishment that follows individual best efforts.
86. I believe in the law of nature.
87. I believe the only way to overcome fear is through knowledge.
88. I believe in the Ten Commandments.
89. I believe there are unjust situations surrounding us and that it is our responsibility to correct them.
90. I believe there is a God and that His plan for all life is more complex than we can yet understand.
91. I believe there is a right and wrong way on the road of life.
92. I believe there is always another option.

93. I believe there is no justification for killing.
94. I believe to be fully alive one must be himself or herself, whatever the cost.
95. I believe true friendship lasts forever.
96. I believe that our pain tells us something, whether good or bad.
97. I believe trust is the basis for all relationships.
98. I believe war does not solve problems.
99. I believe we are all equal in God's eyes.
100. I believe when we stop learning, we invite death, in whatever form it may come.

Your Belief List

1. _____
2. _____
3. _____
4. _____
5. _____
6. _____
7. _____
8. _____
9. _____
10. _____
11. _____
12. _____
13. _____
14. _____
15. _____
16. _____
17. _____
18. _____

PRINCIPLES

"LIVE SO THAT when your children think of fairness and integrity, they think of you," says H. Jackson Brown, Jr., in *Life's Little Instruction Book*.[1]

Fairness and integrity are examples of two wonderful principles. As you travel the road of life, you will need to know which rules to follow. Principles are your rules for life, the ones you have chosen. How do you know which principles you should choose? Remember, the goal of this process is to remove conflict. There are certain laws and principles that exist in nature; gravity is an example. You can't change them, and it would be foolish to live your life trying to change them, or ignoring them. It would create conflicts that could cause you great physical harm. Your Principle List should include all of the rules that you feel you need to follow in order to live your life in alignment with your Belief List.

Is there a perfect list of principles? It really doesn't matter. Your goal should be to develop your own list and continually improve it. Experience will teach you which principles to add, delete, or modify. Why can't you just take someone else's list? You can. However, you will still need to revise it based on your own experience. When your inner blueprint, your written lists, and your actions are in alignment, you will be well on your way to having achieved your goals. You can always test one of your principles by asking yourself if society would be able to prosper with the opposite principle. For example, if honesty is on your list, ask whether society would be able to prosper with dishonesty as one of its core principles? If the answer is no, then your principle is a sound one.

Why do you need to have rules? According to Tom Landry, one of the most successful and highly respected men ever to coach in the National Football League: "Most successful football players not only accept rules and limitations but, I believe, they need them. Players are free to perform at their best only when they know what the expectations are, where the limits stand. I see this as a Biblical principle that also applies to life, a principle our society as a whole has forgotten: you can't enjoy true freedom without limits"[2] Tom Landry's observation is correct. Our children clearly demonstrate this need. They continually test the limits of their environment until they know them and can feel the safety and comfort of those limits.

If people were free to shoot anyone at will, then no one would feel safe on the streets. No one would be truly free. Knowing your limits allows you to live your life within them, resulting in a much fuller and complete life than one in which you were always looking over your shoulder in fear. And you don't have to wonder whether you have done something wrong. This is why children keep testing: They don't want to do anything wrong; they just need to know what is really wrong. So principles serve a valid purpose.

Ben Franklin made the listing and mastering of principles his lifelong project. He called them virtues. Franklin understood that reaching perfection is an arduous task but that ignoring the labor leads to habits (lured by inclination, custom, or the company of others) that are self-destructive.

Here is a sample of a quality Principle List, belonging to Benjamin Franklin.

1. Temperance: *I will* eat not to dullness. *I will* drink not to elevation.
2. Silence: *I will* speak not but what may benefit others or myself. *I will* avoid trifling conversation.

3. Order: *I will* let all my things have their places. *I will* let each part of my business have its time.
4. Resolution: *I will* resolve to perform what I ought. *I will* perform without fail what I resolve.
5. Frugality: *I will* make no expense but to do good to others or myself; i.e., waste nothing.
6. Industry: *I will* lose no time. *I will* be always employed in something useful. *I will* cut off all unnecessary actions.
7. Sincerity: *I will* use no hurtful deceit. *I will* think innocently and justly; and, if I speak, speak accordingly.
8. Justice: *I will* wrong none by doing injuries or omitting the benefits that are my duty.
9. Moderation: *I will* avoid extremes. *I will* forbear resenting injuries so much as I think they deserve.
10. Cleanliness: *I will* tolerate no uncleanness in body, clothes, or habitation.
11. Tranquillity: *I will* be not disturbed at trifles or at accidents common or unavoidable.
12. Chastity: *I will* rarely use venery but for health or offspring—never to dullness, weakness, or the injury of my own or another's peace or reputation.
13. Humility: *I will* imitate Jesus and Socrates.

It is important to understand that becoming the best you are capable of becoming is the goal, not perfection. I believe that humans *are* capable of perfection. Unfortunately, the difficulty in achieving it causes people to shun the idea, withdraw from even trying, and eventually, to develop defense mechanisms that ultimately become self-destructive.

So, though becoming the best you are capable of is the goal, you must continue to strive beyond that goal for perfection. This is the same concept that allows martial arts experts to break the board they are hitting by focusing on a point past the board. It is perfection that leads you to your goal and sometimes beyond it! These principles are the signposts that you will use to help you make decisions when you come to the forks in the road. The principles you select will determine the way you think, act, and react to everything in your life.

A lot of people ask me what the difference is between a belief and a principle. Beliefs refer to the whys, the reasons for doing things in this life; principles to the hows, the ways in which we do things. Principles are the rules we follow while taking some kind of action. Beliefs are the reasons we follow our principles. If one of my beliefs is the Golden Rule, I could select the principle, I will not steal. That principle would be supported by my belief, since I do not want anyone to steal from me. Without the belief to support the rule, I would steal whenever it was to my benefit.

On your list you may have selected reliability as one of your principles. If so, when you start thinking about doing something, you will make sure it does not conflict with something else you have already committed to do. When you commit to doing something, people can count on you not only to be there but to be on time. When someone points out to you that you are late, you no longer get mad at them for their impudent remark but rather thank them and apologize for your tardiness.

Think of yourself walking on the path of life. Your Principle List is like a shield that protects you from people and events that would come along and push you off the path. The temptations that would have otherwise diverted you from your course are too weak to penetrate the shield. The farther along the path you travel, the stronger your shield becomes. One day, your inner blueprint and your daily behavior will be in complete alignment. That will be the day you stop working on your Life Map because you will be living it. That day you will have become the person you have always wanted to be. No longer will others be able to influence you. No longer will your needs and wants battle for your attention. No longer will you worry about pleasing someone else or fear that you have broken some rule or law. You will now be living up to your

own inner blueprint and that is a higher standard than any
you will have faced here on earth. You will be at peace with
the rest of creation.

Responsibility

You can't delegate your responsibility for keeping your actions in alignment with your principles. You are responsible for
your actions. It is possible for others to help you in your efforts
to improve. Sharing your principles with caring friends and rel-
atives puts them in a position of giving you feedback. When
they inform you that your actions are in conflict with your ideal
behavior, you then have the opportunity to make the necessary
corrections. Ultimately, you will consciously choose your actions and thus define the person you are; however, the help you
will receive from caring friends and family will speed the
process.

Principles can and should become habits. When a principle
is so ingrained into your nature that you would not knowingly
or willingly violate it, it has become a habit. Habits are formed
by repetitive action.

Work to improve your thoughts; they ultimately lead to
your behavior.

> We sow our thoughts,
>   and we reap our actions.
> We sow our actions,
>   and we reap our habits.
> We sow our habits,
>   and we reap our character.
> We sow our character,
>   and we reap our destiny.
>
> —ANONYMOUS[3]

Observing yourself successfully conforming to your Principle List is very important. It will lead to the repetition of successes which will become the habitual behaviors that will define you. Benjamin Franklin rotated the thirteen principles on his list every month. He also shared his list with a friend who helped him add to it. Only Franklin can describe the addition:

> My list of virtues contained at first but twelve. But a Quaker friend having kindly informed me that I was generally thought proud, that my pride showed itself frequently in conversation, that I was not content with being in the right when discussing any point, but was over-bearing and rather insolent—of which he convinced me by mentioning several instances—I determined endeavoring to cure myself if I could of this vice or folly among the rest, and I added *Humility* to my list, giving an extensive meaning to the word. I cannot boast of much success in acquiring the *reality* of this virtue, but I had a good deal with regard to the *appearance* of it. [Emphasis in original][4]

Each month he recorded his actions involving that month's principle. He continued the process for over fifty years. He lived his principles!

The early-twentieth-century poet Edgar A. Guest wrote a poem expressing his philosophy, his version of a Principle List:

My Creed

To live as gently as I can;
To be, no matter where, a man;
To take what comes of good or ill
And cling to faith and honor still;
To do my best, and let that stand
The record of my brain and hand;
And then, should failure come to me,
Still work and hope for victory.

To have no secret place wherein
I stoop unseen to shame or sin;
To be the same when I'm alone
As when my every deed is known;
To live undaunted, unafraid
Of any step that I have made;
To be without pretense or sham
Exactly what men think I am.

To leave some simple mark behind
To keep my having lived in mind;
If enmity to aught I show,
To be an honest, generous foe,
To play my little part, nor whine
That greater honors are not mine.
This, I believe, is all I need
For my philosophy and creed.[5]

The rules Guest established for his life were simple, honest, and unassuming. They would be the cause for sound sleep and a peace in passing from this earth. He is a good example of someone who developed rules for his life that expressed his inner blueprint.

Ethics

Some people are becoming more and more concerned with morals and ethics. It is a natural response to the breakdown in our society. Ken Copper, Ph.D., wrote an article in the *Journal of the American Society of CLU & ChFC* entitled, "Rediscovering Ethics: Back to Basics." Michael Joseph Josephson founded the Josephson Institute in an effort to improve the ethical landscape of our American society. As we approach the twenty-first century, the need to deal with these questions is intensifying. Many people are recognizing that the basic principles our society lives by are in desperate need of correction. Each of us must take responsibility for our own conduct. As Tom Hanks recently put it, "The only way you can truly control how you are seen is by being honest all the time."[6]

Honesty includes being honest with ourselves. According to author Michael Levine, "The lies we tell ourselves are more pernicious than the lies we tell others; 'I'm nothing like my mother'. . . . 'I'm too busy to exercise'. . . . 'I don't need therapy'. . . . 'I don't want to get married.' "[7] These simple statements speak volumes. Don't live by someone else's rules; develop your own Principle List and live by it. Every time one person does this, there is one less person supporting the problem. Yes, supporting the problem. Destructive behavior is more acceptable if large numbers of people are involved. The smaller the percentage of the population demonstrating such behavior, the more conspicuous they become. So you are either part of the solution or you are part of the problem. Be part of the solution!

Rabbi Marc Gellman and Monsignor Thomas Hartman state in their book *How Do You Spell God?*:

> All religions teach us to help people whenever we can. All religions teach us to play fair and not to hit or kill or steal or cheat. All religions teach us we should be forgiving and cut people some slack when they mess up, because someday we will mess up too. All religions teach us to love our families, to respect our parents and to make new families when we grow up. Religions all over the world teach the same right way to live.[8]

Every religion teaches principles that could be added to our lists. Don't overlook any source; just remember that you need to filter these principles through your own inner blueprint before you add them to your list.

A definition of a principle: "a rule or a standard, especially of good behavior." If you believe that a principle should be followed and it is supported by one or more of your beliefs, you should add it to your Principle List. For the sake of clarity, identify the belief or beliefs that support each of the principles on your list. You can consider your list complete when you can point to one of your principles as the guiding force in every major decision you have ever made and can conceive of making in the figure. See Suggested Reading at the end of the book to help you with this activity.

It is helpful to begin each principle with the words "I will." Work to limit the number of principles stated negatively. Consider what you will do rather than what you will *not* do. Positive statements are more powerful motivators. Rather than depriving yourself, you will be taking charge of your life. There will be times when you will feel compelled to use the "not" word; referring to the use of drugs might be one of those times. Just keep the use of that word to a minimum.

Retired General H. Norman Schwarzkopf, of Gulf War fame, says, "The truth of the matter is that you always know the right thing to do. The hard part is doing it."[9] Having a written list helps us to remember what to do. How many principles should you have? As many as it takes to provide you with a rule for dealing with all of the major decisions in your life. Remember, each principle should be supported by one or more of your beliefs. Write down your list, now! Here is a list of sample principles from my past Life Mapping students.

Sample Principles

1. I will live with integrity, especially when most unpopular.
2. I will accept responsibility for my actions.
3. I will accept that no one person can change everything.
4. I will accept that some things cannot be repaired or replaced.
5. I will acknowledge and help others maximize their capacity to do good.
6. I will allow myself to make mistakes and will learn from them.
7. I will always be there for my family.

8. I will always keep improving myself.
9. I will seek to understand before being understood.
10. I will be an example of the value of hard work.
11. I will be aware of what is happening in our world.
12. I will be helpful and kind.
13. I will be honest.
14. I will be independent and self-reliant.
15. I will be loyal.
16. I will be patient.
17. I will take immediate action upon my decisions.
18. I will be unique.
19. I will challenge myself.
20. I will change those things that I believe are wrong.
21. I will remain chaste until marriage.
22. I will consider the consequences of my actions before I act.
23. I will control my actions.
24. I will defend others if their rights are being violated.
25. I will enjoy life rather than whine about those things that have gone wrong.
26. I will express myself.
27. I will be fair.
28. I will figure out what my pain is trying to tell me.
29. I will find reason and purpose, no matter how simple, in all that I do.
30. I will forgive and forget.
31. I will strive for greatness.
32. I will have a strong family that will contribute positively to society.
33. I will have confidence in my ability to teach and learn.

34. I will help others as much as I can.
35. I will demonstrate initiative.
36. I will be an example of a person with integrity.
37. I will avoid things that I may become addicted to in a wrong way.
38. I will keep learning.
39. I will keep my promises.
40. I will keep things in perspective.
41. I will laugh often.
42. I will lead rather than follow.
43. I will let people work through their problems, and offer support.
44. I will listen to others.
45. I will live a balanced life.
46. I will live by the Golden Rule.
47. I will look at the bigger picture.
48. I will look for solutions to my problems.
49. I will love and value all people.
50. I will make friends.
51. I will make happiness a factor in decision making.
52. I will make the most of my educational opportunity.
53. I will be a positive role model for my children.
54. I will not abuse my privileges.
55. I will not allow others to control my life.
56. I will take chances.
57. I will not be dependent upon others.
58. I will not be judgmental.
59. I will not be prejudiced.
60. I will not be selfish or greedy.
61. I will not blame others for my mistakes.
62. I will not change my beliefs or principles for money or the threat of violence.
63. I will not change my beliefs to fit the opinions of others.

64. I will not cover up my problems.
65. I will have an open mind.
66. I will not exploit others.
67. I will not fear death.
68. I will not give in to peer pressure.
69. I will not isolate myself from others, even
 when I don't agree with them.
70. I will not kill.
71. I will not let emotions rule my better
 judgment.
72. I will not neglect my beliefs for short-term
 gain.
73. I will not overvalue my possessions.
74. I will not try to control every situation.
75. I will not use fear to my advantage.
76. I will not use lack of support as an excuse not
 to accomplish my goals.
77. I will obey the laws.
78. I will persevere in all that I do.
79. I will be poised.
80. I will pray or commune with God every day.
81. I will protect my family.
82. I will put little value on physical beauty.
83. I will question my actions.
84. I will recognize my capabilities and fulfill
 them.
85. I will relax and be myself.
86. I will remember that everyone makes
 mistakes.
87. I will respect my family.
88. I will inspire others.
89. I will respect others and their property.
90. I will search for my purpose by expanding on
 different possibilities.
91. I will seek and give knowledge, compassion,
 and love.
92. I will seek happiness in all circumstances.
93. I will share.

94. I will be wise with my money and spend it only on things that are necessities.
95. I will spend time alone.
96. I will support punishment for wrongdoing.
97. I will have discipline in my routine.
98. I will be true to myself.
99. I will trust others.
100. I will try my best.

Your Principle List

1. _____
2. _____
3. _____
4. _____
5. _____
6. _____
7. _____
8. _____
9. _____
10. _____
11. _____
12. _____
13. _____
14. _____
15. _____
16. _____
17. _____
18. _____

GOALS

GOALS ARE the destinations we have chosen to work toward. They are the visions we create that we believe are worthy of our attention and effort. The Belief List and Principle List we created in the last two chapters are the foundation upon which we will build our goals. We should not have a goal that conflicts with anything on either of those two lists. Some people say they don't have any goals. What they mean is that they can't see a way of achieving their dreams. Turning a dream into a goal or a vision requires planning and a willingness to follow through on those plans. Anyone can; not everyone will.

Some people don't think they need to write down their goals because they already know what they want and they are surely doing all that they can to make it happen. Some of those same people will tell you that their families are more important than money. Unfortunately, their actions may not support this belief. They work long hours and sacrifice many family activities in order to earn money. They justify it by pointing to the material things they are providing their families. They treat the people at work with respect, then come home and are impatient and irritable with the ones they love. All the while, their family is growing further and further apart. Years later they wonder why their families didn't adequately appreciate all that they had done.

People who focus on the past or their current problems create more of the same. People who focus on their future begin to create that future. The underlying theme behind goal setting is gaining control of your life. Determine what you want; don't let others limit you with their expectations. You can exceed any of their expectations. Ask yourself, if for the moment failure were impossible, what would you want? What are your special gifts?

What Are Our Limitations?

When people think about goals, they usually come face-to-face with their perceived limitations. Instead of thinking about your limitations, the potential problems, or the negative results that might occur, think about the rewards to be gained with reaching each new goal. The gains waiting for those willing to reach their potential far outweigh the risks involved. Don't let the problems keep you from seeing the possibilities.

One woman saw the possibilities and worked to make her dreams into her reality. She was the first woman to run for the presidency of the United States. Belva Ann Lockwood ran twice, in 1884 and 1888. She decided to do so even though women didn't have the right to vote. How is that for a goal! She didn't stop at that. She earned a law degree and became one of the first women to practice law. It didn't end there. She forced an act of Congress to enable her to practice before the U.S. Supreme Court. What goals would inspire you, put a fire in your soul? Have you been afraid to acknowledge them? Think about Belva Ann Lockwood, and start living your dreams! Doing nothing provides its own share of risk.

How close have you come to achieving your potential? What goals will test your perceived limits and bring your achievements closer to your potential? Don't be afraid of exploring new horizons. Overcome the temptation to maintain the status quo; seek the adventure and happiness that awaits you along the path. While writing down your goals will not guarantee success, if followed by the action steps that will be developed in the next chapter, it will put the odds overwhelmingly in your favor. Remember the Harvard study that was mentioned earlier, in which only 3 percent of the students questioned had defined written goals. You will be in rare company.

President Theodore Roosevelt was one of this country's greatest advocates of going for your goals. "Far better is to dare mighty things," he said, "to win glorious triumphs, even though checkered by failure, than take rank with those poor spirits who neither enjoy much nor suffer much, because they live in the gray twilight that knows not victory nor defeat."[1]

Of course, before you can dare mighty things, you have to decide what mighty things you will dare. The noise and confusion you live in may make that a difficult task. But the glorious triumphs will be worth the sacrifice. So now is the time to find a quiet place, away from all distractions. You think you are too busy to take a break. This is a common feeling. The reality is that you are too busy not to take a break. Some of those things that are keeping you busy are not necessary. Only by taking the time to determine your real priorities will you be able to eliminate the unnecessary ones. You might find that you were creating some of the noise in an effort to prevent yourself from feeling the pain associated with discovering how much you disliked those unnecessary activities. Whatever time it takes, the results will be worth it, in the long run.

Goals Need to Be Balanced

The act of deciding on our goals is a very important step. Our lives actually become the goals we are actively pursuing. As James Allen says, "Until thought is linked with purpose there is no intelligent accomplishment. With most people, the bark of thought is allowed to drift upon the ocean of life. . . . We need to conceive of a legitimate purpose in our heart, and set out to accomplish it."[2] Proper goal setting is a process in which your beliefs and your principles meld to form a list of goals. Others may witness your growth, but you alone will live it. The life you have chosen begins when you link your thoughts with your purpose. One obstacle in achieving the life we want is lack of balance. Visualize a chair with four legs. If one of the legs is removed, what happens to the chair? This very same principle applies to our lives. When one area of our life is neglected, we begin to sense the uneasy feeling of falling. Someone so devoted to their work that they neglect their family will one day regret the imbalance that causes them to lose their family. To achieve a balanced life, we need to have goals in the four basic areas of life:

- Spiritual, that part of us that understands the real meaning of our lives and helps us connect with the rest of creation and beyond
- Physical, the care we give to the vessel we will use for our journey on earth
- Familial, the way we relate to and interact with our family
- Societal, all of our interaction with the rest of creation, including your career

Forsaking the physical for any of the other areas would lead us to ill health or death. We certainly can't be at our best in the other areas if this happens. Balance is the key to reaching our true potential as a "whole" being, becoming fully human. The dictionary tells us that the word "whole" means containing all parts, not being disjointed. Reaching our full potential requires all four of our parts.

The four areas are listed in the order of priority. The Pyramid of Personal Development on the next page shows the relationship of the four areas. The center is your spiritual development. If your spirit is weak, you will be unknowingly led to a life of destruction and misery, and unable to work on any of your other areas.

Moving outward, if you are physically weaker than you could be, you will be less able to work on the other areas. These first two areas make it possible to work on the last two. However, no spiritual, physical, career, or community successes will compensate you for the loss of your family. To be whole, we need to keep our lives complete, and in balance.

"My object in living is to unite my avocation and my voca-

THE PYRAMID OF
PERSONAL DEVELOPMENT

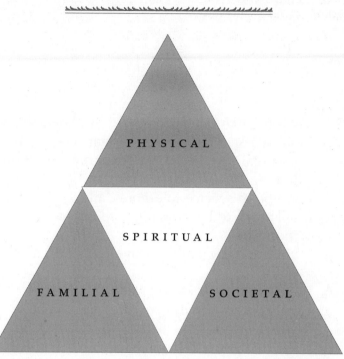

tion as my two eyes make one in sight. Only where love and need are one . . . and work is play for mortal stakes is the deed ever really done for heaven and the future's sake," stated the poet Robert Frost.[3] To accomplish this worthy goal, we need to start asking ourselves simple questions. Answer the following questions, for each of the four basic areas of your life—spiritual, familial, societal, and physical: "What is my ideal vision of the person I want to become? How do I want to be remembered?"

Spiritual: Your vision might include any or many of the following: developing your relationship with God, living in harmony with nature, learning to understand yourself through meditation, connecting with the universal consciousness, developing your higher powers, understanding your subconscious, discovering cycles and how we fit into them, or clarifying your concept of how life began. This is not a complete list; it is intended to spark your imagination. Here are some sample spiritual goals from my students.

Sample Spiritual Goals

1. I will baptize my children before they are one.
2. I will work to be more confident when I speak, and realize when it is appropriate beginning today.
3. I will be of service to others daily.
4. I will work to become more self-confident monthly.
5. I will bring joy through love to those I meet daily.
6. I will build my own morality this year.
7. I will continually live my life as if someone was watching me beginning today.
8. I will define my relationship with the power greater than myself this year.
9. I will develop myself in preparation for this battle of survival of the fittest beginning today.
10. I will discuss God with my children weekly and help them develop their understanding of him.
11. I will explore other churches monthly.
12. I will find my twin soul before I die.
13. I will form an opinion about life after death this year.
14. I will give my children the freedom to find their own way of worshiping God every day.
15. I will go to heaven when I die.
16. I will grow old gracefully beginning today.
17. I will harmonize my actions with my beliefs; I won't patronize companies whose policies I disagree with, starting today.

18. I will improve my inner beauty as opposed to my outer beauty daily.
19. I will keep my spiritual soul healthy beginning today.
20. I will better know God each day.
21. I will learn more about religion each month.
22. I will learn my life partner's religion before we get married.
23. I will learn to accept others through understanding of them and their culture daily.
24. I will learn to be more myself each month.
25. I will learn to give more of myself every day.
26. I will learn to love others this year.
27. I will learn to meditate this year.
28. I will learn to think more like Jesus when making decisions, beginning today.
29. I will learn to better understand and obey God's will each year.
30. I will learn yoga next month.
31. I will live my life looking to the future, rather than back at the past beginning today.
32. I will live a life that is loyal and true to God every day.
33. I will love God every day.
34. I will begin today to develop the feeling of inner peace.
35. I will meditate daily.
36. I will pray daily.
37. I will read a book every month to develop my spirit.
38. I will read about life after death this month.
39. I will read Bible stories to my children Sunday evenings.
40. I will see people who are foreign to me with a more open mind beginning today.
41. I will seek a formal means of religious expression this year.
42. I will study Christianity more next year.

43. I will take at least 10 minutes daily to reflect on my day.
44. I will begin taking my children to Sunday school next week.
45. I will bond spiritually weekly with my friends.
46. I will better understand who God is every month.
47. I will better understand who I am every month.
48. I will volunteer to teach and sing in church choir next month.
49. I will work at a soup kitchen monthly.
50. I will work in community service to help the less fortunate weekly.

Physical: Your vision might include: discovering the ideal exercise, diet, or weight, or developing lifestyle habits that promote longevity: getting adequate sleep, eating breakfast daily, avoiding tobacco, or moderating alcohol. Here are some sample physical goals from my students.

Sample Physical Goals

1. I will maintain an acceptable diet, daily.
2. I will exercise three times a week.
3. I will maintain an acceptable weight, daily.
4. I will drink 8 glasses of water daily for 21 days to make it a habit.
5. I won't smoke.
6. I will avoid drugs.
7. I won't drink.
8. I will take a self-defense class within the next six months.
9. I won't eat pork.
10. I will do 100 push-ups, sit-ups, kick-outs a day.
11. I will ride horses weekly.

12. I will golf weekly.
13. I will walk daily.
14. I will ride my bike three times a week.
15. I will play soccer weekly.
16. I will play three sets of tennis three times a week.
17. I will hike for 30 minutes three times a week.
18. I will play basketball for one hour twice a week.
19. I will play baseball weekly.
20. I will Rollerblade for 30 minutes three times a week.
21. I will lose 10 pounds within six months.
22. I will eat three servings of fruit daily.
23. I will swim 2 laps a day.
24. I will be a vegetarian for the next 12 months.
25. I will participate in the Bay to Breakers [an annual six-mile race in San Francisco] next year.
26. I will exercise 20 minutes a day.
27. I will run 30 minutes a day.
28. I will improve my muscle mass over the summer.
29. I will eliminate junk food from my diet starting today.
30. I will consult a physician this month about my exercise program.
31. I will consult a dietician about my diet this month.
32. I will take a nutrition class this year and learn how food relates to my health.
33. I will have a yearly physical.
34. I will take a stress reduction class this year and integrate it into my lifestyle.
35. I will work with a personal trainer to develop a weekly workout routine.
36. I will do tai chi chuan for 30 minutes daily.
37. I will sleep at least 8 hours nightly.
38. I will take vitamins daily.
39. I will weigh myself daily.

40. I will get a massage weekly.
41. I will strengthen my back through weekly exercise.
42. I will stretch daily to maintain flexibility.
43. I will use my family history to develop a preventive health program this year.
44. I will do yoga exercises for 30 minutes three times a week.
45. I will work out with my workout tape three times a week.
46. I will listen to my subliminal weight-loss tape daily.
47. I will take a 15-minute meditation break daily.
48. I will train for and complete a marathon within the next year.
49. I will bench-press two hundred pounds by the end of the summer.
50. I will hit a golf ball 300 yards before the end of the year.

Familial: Your vision might include: the kind of spouse, parent, sibling, or child you could become. How would you act in each of these relationships? What kinds of things would you enjoy doing in these roles? How would you feel as a result of these changes? Are you living within your budget or do you need to work on it? Here are some sample familial goals of past students.

Sample Familial Goals

1. I will find my lifelong companion before I marry.
2. I will make special time for my spouse daily.
3. I will teach my children daily all of the positive things my parents taught me by setting a good example.

4. I will be a good mother every day and enjoy my children in the process.
5. I will learn to communicate with every member of my family within six months.
6. I will learn to respect my family daily.
7. I will love and care for my family daily.
8. I will be involved in family activity weekly.
9. I will write my grandparents meaningful letters and send them cards at least twice every month.
10. I will help any family member in need and inquire about needs weekly.
11. I will learn to manage money within three months.
12. I will have or adopt children after I marry.
13. I will improve my family environment weekly.
14. I will play tennis weekly with my father.
15. I will read to my children for 30 minutes every night.
16. I will work weekly to understand my parents' decisions.
17. I will help my family achieve their goals and inquire weekly about them.
18. I will attend every school and sports event my child is in that I can this year.
19. I will help my brother gain more independence within the next twelve months.
20. I will start today to plan to provide the financial resources to allow my children to attend college.
21. I will learn to listen to my family more fully by the end of the year.
22. I will help my parents with chores daily.
23. I will cut out silly stories from magazines and newspapers and send them to my mom in a package of love monthly.
24. I will maintain a close relationship with my brother by calling him twice a

month to touch base and give him sisterly
    advice.
25. I will help my family financially this year.
26. I will learn to appreciate and respect both my
    father and stepfather this year.
27. I will eat dinner with the whole family weekly.
28. I will help my children graduate from high
    school in four years.
29. I will participate in a weekly family council
    meeting.
30. I will thank someone in the family for
    something nice they did for me weekly.
31. I will spend time with my grandparents
    weekly.
32. I will take time weekly to improve my
    relationships with different family members.
33. I will get to know my children's friends daily.
34. I will make sure that I offer my support and
    friendship daily.
35. I will work to minimize my need for help from
    my family this year.
36. I will play cards with my grandpa weekly.
37. I will remember all of my family's special
    days.
38. I will design and implement a retirement plan
    this year.
39. I will develop and implement a budget next
    month.
40. I will get custody of and raise my sons this
    year.
41. I will coach my children in sports this year.
42. I will see my brother in at least one college
    basketball game this year.
43. I will take my aunt in Los Angeles to lunch or
    dinner at least once every six months.
44. I will support my children in all positive
    activities daily.

45. I will work daily to help my children graduate
    from college.
46. I will help my children daily find their
    purpose in life and support their endeavors
    to succeed in that purpose.
47. I will try to maintain an atmosphere of
    happiness in our home daily.
48. I will call my parents and grandparents twice
    a month for at least 20 minutes of heartfelt
    conversation.
49. I will develop a relationship with my
    grandchildren by seeing them once a week
    to have fun.
50. I will organize a family reunion once every
    five years to keep in touch with extended
    family.

Societal: You will spend more time in your vocation than in
any other activity you will participate in, except sleeping. Make
sure that you don't choose the wrong career for the wrong reason.
Too many people get up each day and drag themselves to a job to
make a living. Ask yourself, "If we lived in a world without
money, what would I be doing?" Don't settle for an unfulfilling
career in exchange for financial rewards. You will be sentencing
yourself to years of frustration. By carefully assessing your gifts,
interests, and principles, you will be able to identify career opportunities that will bring you the most satisfaction. Make this choice
your passion. Listen to Robert Frost: "where your love and need
are one." Finding your passion, something you would love doing,
is the first step in deciding on a career. Don't settle for someone
else's passion or let someone else define your limitations.

There is a little book called *The Animal School,* by Dr. R. H.
Reeves, about a school attended by different kinds of animals. The
school decided to test the animals in a number of different areas.
One particular duck, an excellent swimmer and flier, turned out
to be a very poor runner, so in their infinite wisdom, the school
officials decided that the duck could no longer swim or fly until

he improved his running. Soon he became an average runner, but for some unexplained reason, he became only an average swimmer and flier.[4] Don't let anyone influence you into giving up the things at which you excel! Do you need additional education? If the answer is yes, then make that a goal! Always allow your creativity to work for you. There is life after vocation, even a fulfilling one.

Don't forget to include your friends. "When you stop spending time with real friends, you lose your balance,"[5] says Michael Levine in *Lessons at the Halfway Point*. The rest of your vision might include: travel, your involvement with politics, civic organizations, charities, etc.

Here are some sample societal goals of past Life Mappers.

Sample Societal Goals

1. I will find a career that involves tasks which I love doing before I graduate.
2. I will work weekly on seeing people from the inside not outside.
3. I will learn other languages and cultures annually.
4. I will volunteer weekly at a local hospital.
5. I will work weekly on trusting people and contributing to others.
6. I will vote in every election.
7. I will work weekly on learning to communicate effectively without hurting others.
8. I will invest $1,000 in a mutual fund this year.
9. I will work monthly on increasing the number of and quality of my friendships.
10. I will work daily on never being afraid to express my opinion.
11. I will be involved in my community weekly.
12. I will travel to Africa and live with an indigenous culture within three years.

13. I will work toward a degree in social work within six years.
14. I will write a real magazine for young women within ten years.
15. I will become a doctor in eight years.
16. I will become a journalist in six years.
17. I will earn a master's degree in six years.
18. I will become a computer engineer in four years.
19. I will enjoy my friends daily.
20. I will travel to every continent within twenty years.
21. I will open an IRA with $500 this year and add $250 yearly for 15 years.
22. I will create a student center by graduation.
23. I will complete all of my homework daily.
24. I will join a service club this year.
25. I will take a class next month to further my job possibilities.
26. I will go to a career counselor this month to improve my career.
27. I will volunteer 100 hours annually to community service.
28. I will bungee jump with a friend this year.
29. I will go back to school this year to get my two-year nursing degree.
30. I will become a professional soccer player within four years.
31. I will become an actor by age 30.
32. I will donate money weekly to the needy.
33. I will volunteer weekly to help others.
34. I will become knowledgeable on controversial issues this year.
35. I will graduate from a college I love by the year 2002.
36. I will tutor children weekly at a local high school.
37. I will volunteer at the library weekly to teach reading.

38. I will volunteer at the children's school
    weekly.
39. I will read the newspaper daily to keep up on
    current events.
40. I will volunteer to drive once a week for Meals
    on Wheels.
41. I will spend time weekly with a close friend.
42. I will take a class this year and read all I can
    about the study of herbs and natural
    medicine.
43. I will join toastmasters and work on my
    speech-giving abilities this year.
44. I will start a frequent flier program this year.
45. I will join a political party and learn more
    about the candidates this year.
46. I will become more politically active this year
    by working to get people registered to vote.
47. I will become a lifetime buddy to someone
    who is HIV-positive this year.
48. I will pay off my home loan in 10 years.
49. I will complete my book and sign a publishing
    contract this year.
50. I will start a 401(k) plan this year and begin
    with a 3 percent contribution and increase it
    by 1 percent every three years.

Back to Your Dreams

A friend of mine, Hal Urban, a teacher and the author of
Life's Greatest Lessons or 20 Things I Want to Know, has his psychology class make a list of one hundred things they would like
to do before they die. It is a very interesting exercise. It can tell
you a lot about your priorities. Take the time to try this exercise
yourself. When you complete the list, identify your top ten and
work them into your future goals list.

What dreams have you had about your life? Make sure that

your dreams are included in the lists you are creating. Take those dreams you are transforming into goals and write a paragraph for each goal that you set. This paragraph should include your reasons for choosing every goal and discuss why the goal is important to you. See yourself already achieving the goal. How do you feel? Write it down! The vision this creates becomes so vivid that it brings your goal to life. It gives you the needed incentive when the going gets rough and you contemplate giving up. You also need to consider the cost you are willing to pay to reach the goal. Do the research necessary to fully determine what will be required for you to accomplish this goal. Include this information in your paragraph. It will allow you to face the cost and change your mind if necessary before you have wasted too much time or money in the pursuit of that goal.

Read these paragraphs as often as possible, and certainly whenever you are frustrated or thinking of giving up on your goal. This activity will bring back the feelings and thought process that you used in creating the goal. It will help you decide whether you need to modify the goal. This is just the beginning of building the vision of the person you want to become. It is how you will proactively manage your life . . . now and into the future. You will modify this vision many times over the years. Experience will make you wiser and your vision will come ever nearer to alignment with your inner blueprint. The nearer you come, the more clearly you will see the overall picture.

As your view of the overall picture becomes clearer, you will find yourself at peace with your world. The better you feel, the more creative you will become. Make sure that you allow your creative side to mature. Give it all the resources necessary to develop. Pure joy will follow and so will the day you truly begin to live your purpose.

Commit It to Writing

Everyone has heard the old saying, "The journey of a thousand miles begins with a single step." It is one thing to understand a concept; it is quite another to take action. It is much easier to strike out on a new trail when you have a guide to lead the way. Developing your goals begins when you commit them to writing. This is the next step in completing your Life Map, your guide to your future! So get out a piece of paper and start writing them down. They need to be specific; your mind cannot deal with generalities. You want a new white Ford Mustang convertible. You need to have a timeline associated with the goal; that is one of the steps in turning a wish into a goal. You want that Mustang by June 1. You also need a plan to accomplish this goal, and you will develop one in the next chapter.

Be Ready for Surprises

Sometimes our goals surprise us. We labor to produce one fruit and end up enjoying a very unexpected and quite different one. I read a story in *Family Circle* about a woman who planted a rose garden. One year she discovered that something very large was eating her roses. She woke up early one morning to find a magnificent deer just ten feet from her window, dining on her Queen Elizabeths. Now each year she is faced with the dilemma of fencing her yard and having a rose garden or spending time watching this magical animal. Her goal was a rose garden. Her surprise was the silence and peacefulness of watching the deer. Look for the mysteries in life and don't be so focused on your goal that you miss the surprise!

A Sample Goal List

Here is a sample of a quality Goal List, from a past Life Mapper:

- Spiritual
    1. Find a church this year.
    2. Spend time alone weekly.

3. Read daily.
4. Share with others weekly.

- Familial goals
    1. Actively participate with my children on special days and weekends.
    2. Communicate with my immediate family weekly.
    3. Develop and live my budget this year.
    4. Begin asking for help immediately when needed.
    5. Finish school this year.
    6. Keep looking for a life partner weekly.

- Physical
    1. Exercise daily.
    2. Cook/eat good food daily.
    3. Plan adventurous activities monthly.

- Societal goals
    1. Explore my career options weekly.
    2. Attend more social activities monthly.
    3. Meet more people/make more friends monthly.

Time to Prioritize

Now that you have some goals identified in each area, you need to prioritize them.

The single most common error in developing goals is over-scheduling. People get caught up in trying to do it all. The result is a schedule that is so full we are stressed most of the time and much less efficient. It is better to start with a few goals and move on to the next goal on the priority list once we have reached one, or find that we have enough extra time in the schedule to add another activity. It is advisable to begin with only one or two goals in each area. Remember, for dreams and wishes to graduate to goals, they must have completion dates. Yes, that ugly word, dead-lines. Deadlines provide the information needed to develop a time-line. That makes your progress measurable and allows you to make the adjustments necessary for the accomplishment of the goal.

What is enough? When you begin to establish goals in dif-ferent areas of your life, think about limits that truly express your idea of what is enough. How much land is enough? How big a house is enough? Do you need to own a vacation home or is renting enough?

During my twenty-one years in the insurance business, I have learned from my policyholders. Life in our modern society has developed into a fairly routine cycle. When we are young, under thirty, we think we are going to live forever; we spend all that we earn and then some, and believe we will have more than enough time to plan for retirement. Between the ages of thirty and fifty, we begin the accumulation stage. We buy houses, fancy cars, art, fine furniture, and designer clothes. Then, between fifty and sixty-five, when the children are grown and have moved out of the house, we start wondering what we are going to do with all this stuff. And so, sometime in our sixties or seventies, we begin to give it away. If we could start the cycles with a better understanding of what is really important to us, we would come to the later stages better prepared. Our preparation would allow us to understand that what we have is not as important as what we have become. The decisions we would make along life's journey would be more in alignment with our blueprint.

As you move along your life path, remember the warning of H. Jackson Browne, Jr., in *Life's Little Instruction Book*: "Don't let your possessions possess you."[6] Things are just that, things. They can be replaced, but people, relationships, your integrity, your character, your health and the many yesterdays we have watched pass away . . . these can't be replaced. Keep your priorities straight.

Listen to what Ralph Fiennes, a two-time Oscar nominee, had to say about success and keeping your priorities straight, in a recent interview in *Parade* magazine: "What's really scary about being in demand is that, when the world decides you're a desirable commodity, you haven't really changed inside. The material rewards are very, very tempting. People think that, to be successful, you've got to take the car, the house, the big fee. They haven't thought about happiness. But recent events in my life have made me ask the question, 'What is the cost?' "

Fiennes explained why his childhood helped him. "It was a very hand-to-mouth existence, there was very little money. My parents were broke. But we did have an environment at home whereby there was always encouragement to do whatever we wanted to do. The strength of my Catholic ethic underpinning everything, the fabric of the family life, was so strong."

When asked about his success, Fiennes replied, "Success? Well, I don't know quite what you mean by success. Material success? Worldly success? Personal, emotional success? The people I consider successful are so because of how they handle their responsibilities to other people, how they approach the future, people who have a full sense of the value of their life and what they want to do with it. I call people 'successful' not because they have money or their business is doing well but because, as human beings, they have a fully developed sense of being alive and are engaged in a lifetime task of collaboration with other human beings—their mothers and fathers, their family, their friends, their loved ones, the friends who are dying, the friends who are being born.

"Success? Don't you know it is all about being able to extend love to people? Really. Not in a big, capital-letter sense but in the everyday. Little by little, task by task, gesture by gesture, word by word. . . . Success? What about Happiness?" Dotson Rader, who interviewed Mr. Fiennes for *Parade*, did a fine job of bringing out Mr. Fiennes's Life Mapping concepts. We should all have our priorities as straight as Ralph Fiennes![7]

The Real Gift in Giving

When you are rushing on to your next goal, excited at the successful completion of a prior one, remember to appreciate the people who have helped you along the way. Look for ways to give back to your community, your family, your friends. That is the best way to ensure the opportunity for a happy life for your progeny. The ultimate result of giving is the unexpected gift we receive, the understanding that we have everything we really want and need. This feeling of abundance will provide you a new freedom as you share your money and your knowledge with those who eagerly await your gift. This act empowers those you have chosen to share yourself with to become greater than they had imagined possible. That happens because you have shown them that someone truly cares, that they are important.

Now, sit down and start writing. Write as many different goals as possible. After you have written them down, prioritize them and select only the top one or two in each of life's four categories to begin working on now. Maintain an active list of goals for future action and continue to prioritize them. You will use them in the future when your schedule permits. Use the paragraphs you have written to help you visualize yourself completing those top one or two goals in each category. This visualization is very important. Your mind will be more focused if it can see you successfully achieving your goal. Keep updating your Goal List. This is just the beginning . . . you will improve this list many times during your life.

A Short Review

This is a good time to review the differences among beliefs, principles, and goals.

Your Belief List represents the universal truths, as you know them. Your behavior is the living example of your Principle List. Goals are things you are attempting to achieve, learn, or acquire.

So, when you look at my Familial Goal List, you will find "facilitate harmony daily." My principle, "I will be cooperative," is supported by my belief, "God wants us to be treated equally." That follows since I want people to cooperate with me; therefore, I should live that example by being cooperative myself. It is not a goal I am trying to achieve; it is a rule I want to live by.

One final example:

Belief—I believe one should follow the laws of the
community they choose to live in.
Principle—I will obey all of the laws when I drive.
Goal—I will drive my car from San Jose to San
Francisco today.

As subtle as these differences sometimes are, it is very
important to understand them as you begin to build your lists.

Your Goal List

Spiritual

1. _____
2. _____
3. _____
4. _____

Physical

1. _____
2. _____
3. _____
4. _____

Familial

1. _____
2. _____
3. _____
4. _____

Societal

1. _____
2. _____
3. _____
4. _____

ACTIVITIES

Wʜᴀᴛ is your purpose? What are you supposed to contribute to this world? How will you ever know if you don't try to fulfill your destiny? What you do every day, the activities, define you and your contribution to this world. Some people mistake activity for achievement. They are so busy doing things, they don't have time to evaluate the results of all that activity. It is not just any activity that leads you to your goals; it is a particular set of activities.

Activities without goals are unproductive drudgery; goals without activities are dreams; when activities and goals are combined everything is possible! Your Belief List tells *why* you are alive, your Goal List tells you *what* you are to do in this life, and your Principle List and Activity List tell you *how* you will get it done. Nothing is accomplished until something is done.

The diagram on the next page shows how beliefs lead to activities. The example used is directly from my own Life Map.

The Puzzle

Goals are like puzzles; activities are like the pieces you use to complete the puzzle, one piece at a time. Take your highest-priority goal and break it into a list of activities that are necessary for the completion of the goal. Make sure you keep breaking

FROM BELIEF TO ACTIVITY

An example

the activities into smaller and smaller pieces, until each individual activity can be completed within a week, or preferably a day. Then take this list of activities and put them in chronological order. Follow this procedure for all of the goals you have selected. Select the correct activities and you will have created your masterpiece, your contribution to this world. "The future," said Walt Disney, "is not the result of choices among alternate paths offered in the present—it is a place that is created—created first in the mind and will; created next in the activity." Listen to the master of imagination. Walt Disney created what others laughed at as impossible.

Andy Granatelli, a giant in the Indy car-racing business, once said, "When you are making a success of something, it's not work. It's a way of life. You enjoy yourself because you are making your contribution to the world." Your contribution!

Love

"Three things are necessary for the salvation of man: to know what he ought to believe, to know what he ought to desire, and to know what he ought to do." This formulation of Life Mapping by Saint Thomas Aquinas over seven hundred years ago helped people understand that believing (a Belief List) and having goals (a Goal List) were only the beginning. You have to do something, you have to actively use your Principle List and your Activity List to assist you in achieving your goals.

Love is the reason this process works. Everything you have done to this point is inspired by your love for the person you want to become. Love creates an attitude that prepares you for the rest of your journey. According to Hyrum W. Smith:

> Love inspires a different kind of behavior than either duty or fear. If I love my work, I don't do it for anyone else. I do it because I love it; I want to do it. I revel in it and, chances are, I will have much success and satisfaction in it. If I love my children instead of fearing for

them, I don't restrict them with unrealistic require-
ments. I trust them. I teach them. And I let them go out
into the great, wide world, prepared and eager to live
their own lives.[1]

Love your life and those you choose to share it with.

My memories of my grandmother are still vivid. She loved
life and shared it with everybody. She created many special adventures for me, which usually centered around the kitchen or
the garden. I really didn't have much interest in either of them;
however, she made them fun. She shared a piece of what she
loved with me and before I knew what had happened, I began
to love being in the kitchen. To this day I still love being in the
kitchen. As my grandmother demonstrated, we are all teachers.
What people will learn from us is a function of who we are and
our observable behavior. It is a rather large responsibility. Few
experiences in life equal the joy of successfully mentoring another person. Both participants in the mentoring process are en-
riched. Whether the person you are mentoring is your own child
or a complete stranger, the rewards will be great. We must each
take whatever time is required to make sure everyone in our
family understands the power of love and that they are loved.
Sharing this with someone outside your family is the next step.

The habits we develop, as we attempt to show our love of
others, can be virtues or vices. When they are in alignment with
our beliefs and support our individual development, they are
virtues. There are two components of Life Mapping, principles
and activities, that can become habits. Repeating principles or
activities that support our purpose will eventually make them
habits and, of course, virtues. If we have taken the time to think
a situation through once, it only makes sense to develop it into
a habit. There is no sense doing the same work twice. Forming
habits frees our mind to work on more creative things. Even
more important, when they become habits, we perform them
more successfully. Work to acquire each habit you desire.

This is the principle at work in athletics. It is why athletes
spend so much time practicing. "We are what we repeatedly do.
Excellence, then, is not an act, but a habit," said Aristotle.

Habit

I am your constant companion.
I am your greatest helper or heaviest burden.
I will push you onward or drag you down to failure.
I am completely at your command.
Half the things you do you might just as well
turn over to me and I will be able to do them
quickly and correctly.
I am easily managed—
you must merely be firm with me.
Show me exactly how you want
something done and after a few lessons
I will do it automatically.
I am the servant of all great men;
and alas, of all failures, as well.
Those who are great, I have made great.
Those who are failures, I have made failures.
I am not a machine,
though I work with all the precision
of a machine plus the intelligence of a man.
You may run me for a profit or run me for ruin—
it makes no difference to me.
Take me, train me, be firm with me,
and I will place the world at your feet.
Be easy with me and I will destroy you.
Who am I? I am habit!

—ANONYMOUS[2]

Parameters Can Influence Results

   The achievement of goals will require more than the identi-
fying of activities and the completion of those activities. You
will also need to know the parameters that define your ability
to achieve the goal. So, this would include thinking about
whether you need a special environment, lighting, music, food,

etc.; the number of hours per week you will need to be success-ful; whose help you will need. Defining the parameters provides the limits necessary for deciding on the activities required to accomplish your goals. This is the first step in determining activities.

Free Yourself from Past Mistakes

When your behavior or activities are in conflict with your purpose, the correct response is to acknowledge it, devise a plan to minimize the possibility of repeating such conflict, and then forget about it. Don't spend another minute thinking about it. It is history. Listen to Ralph Waldo Emerson on the subject: "Fin-ish every day and be done with it. You have done what you could. Some blunders and absurdities no doubt crept in; forget them as soon as you can. Tomorrow is a new day; begin it well and serenely and with too high a spirit to be encumbered with your old nonsense. This day is all that is good and fair. It is too dear, with its hopes and invitations, to waste a moment on the yesterdays."[3]

Enjoy the Journey

The Activity List you create for your goals will change as you face the choices that life will bring. Don't get stuck on the activities; keep the goal in mind. When you plan and review each week, you will have the opportunity to change your activi-ties as needed to reach your goals. Remember, you are doing these activities out of love, not fear or duty! Learn to enjoy the activities required to reach your goal. If you don't enjoy the ac-tivity, search for an alternate one that you do enjoy that will lead to the achievement of the goal.

These activities are the roads that lead you to your destina-tion, and there is always a scenic road somewhere. Think of the beautiful, enjoyable alternate choice as taking the more scenic road to Grandma's house. You still get there, maybe a few minutes later, but you enjoyed the trip. Goals are like long journeys completed one step or activity at a time.

When my son was young, one of his heroes was He-Man. He is a fictional character in the *Masters of the Universe* cartoon strip. Hollywood decided to make a movie to capitalize on the popularity of the cartoon. Of course, my son and I went to see the movie. We enjoyed it. Near the end someone is celebrating the moment of victory over the evil Skelator when He-Man responds, "Live the journey, for the destination is but the doorway to the next journey!"

Suddenly, I realized that he had summarized life. We are here to reach destinations and fulfill our purpose, but we are supposed to enjoy doing it. Begin to look at things as if you had never seen them before or that you might never see them again. Cultivate your senses. Learn to appreciate the subtle nuances. Can you smell the fresh bread baking? Savor the moments. Did you hear the children laughing in the park? Instead of hurrying through lunch, make it an experience. Eat with a friend or try a new restaurant or discover a special spot in your home. Make the selection of the food interesting; try new combinations of tastes. Think about the wonderful tastes and the magic of seed, soil, sun, and water that made it all possible. Soon it will become an event you look forward to. Take the time to plan and make it more than just eating. Read a little poetry or a fun book. Smell the flowers along the way, feel the sunshine on your face, watch the squirrel race up the tree, and listen to the leaves crunch under your feet.

Those who contemplate the beauty this world holds for us will find a sense of peace and strength that will endure a lifetime. Drink in the wonder that surrounds you. Don't let the vision of the goal spoil the joy to be found in the activities.

Enjoying the activities might sound strange to someone who is doing something they don't like. Most important, you should not be doing something you don't like. Get rid of that job and find a rewarding career, one that brings you joy! This is not a rehearsal, this is your life. Make it fun. Find a career that is fun. What if you have obligations that make leaving your job difficult? Plan for the transition to your career. For some this might require several years. The years will pass whether you plan or not. You might as well do the planning and be in a position to make the transition when the time is right. Of course, finding a career is part of the goal setting process and, hopefully, you have resolved that issue in the last chapter.

Delegation

Now what do you do about those activities you don't like doing that are required in your career? You learn to delegate them to other people. You don't think they can do them as well as you can? Then teach them, have confidence in them, and take every opportunity to encourage and congratulate them. It isn't a complicated process. You explain their responsibilities in enough detail to allow them to complete the activity. Make sure they know you have confidence in their ability to successfully complete the activity and give them the authority to successfully accomplish it.

There is nothing more frustrating than being given a task and not the authority to accomplish it. For example, if you asked your employee to reorganize a filing system without giving him the authority to buy the needed supplies, every time he found he was short something he would have to come to you for permission to buy it. That would show that you didn't trust his judgment and would weaken his confidence for future decisions. However, if you gave him the authority to buy whatever he needed, he would complete the task and be ready for the next one.

After a task is completed, you need to compliment him on the work he completed successfully and explain any areas that he could improve on next time. "Over the years I have become convinced that every detail is important and that success usually accompanies attention to little details," says John Wooden, the most successful college basketball coach, ever, in his book *They Call Me Coach*. "It is this, in my judgment, that makes for the difference between champion and near champion."[4]

To illustrate the impact that John Wooden has had on UCLA basketball, listen to what a current player, Cameron Dollar, was quoted saying some twenty years after Wooden's retirement: "Repetition is what gives you confidence; keep working and good things happen."[5]

Pay attention to the details. Soon those marvelous people you have delegated to, will be doing those things better than you could. Especially since you don't like doing them.

Fun and Focus

There are some activities you can't delegate. This is where that wonderful imagination you were given comes into play. Play is the operational word. Remember, never lose sight of the goal; however, if you are certain that an activity is part of reaching the goal, you need to develop ways to make the activity fun. Turn it into a game, time yourself, add minor challenges into the activity. If your activity is calling customers to check on their satisfaction with a service, see how many you can make laugh during the call. Keep track. Put a score sheet on your desk and set your record for most laughing calls in an hour.

Make your work area as pleasant a place to be as possible. If you like flowers or family pictures, place them where they can add pleasure to your day. Suddenly, the calling will become a game and you will begin having fun. The hour will pass much more quickly. Another key point to activities is that they require you to focus. If you are to maximize the results achieved in reaching your goal, you must maximize the results for each activity. Once you are performing an activity, forget about the goal; you will think about the goal when you plan and review each week, so focus on the activity. The more often you successfully perform the activity, the easier it becomes to repeat that success.

Southwest Airlines ran a television ad recently featuring a dog, his bone, and the concept of focusing. The ad incites you to focus on their message by repeatedly using the phrase "find the bone." Each time they insert a picture of the dog finding a bone. Of course, they are hoping you are focusing on their airline's benefits at the same time.

Focusing and being able to successfully repeat an action is what athletes call entering "the zone." When you are in the zone, you don't need to think about each step in the activity; you just need to keep focused. Don't let anything distract you. The best way to get an athlete out of their zone is to disrupt their concentration. That is why teams call time-out just before a key field goal is to be kicked or a key free throw is about to be shot. They want the person attempting the activity to have time to think about other things; maybe a doubt will sneak in to disrupt his focus.

So have fun and focus; every activity you are doing is the most important one you have to do at that time, or you would be doing something else. Stay focused and give every activity your best effort.

Goals and Activities

Here is the sample of a quality Goal List (see the discussion of goals in Chapter 5):

- Spiritual goals
    1. Find a church this year.
    2. Spend time alone weekly.
    3. Read daily.
    4. Share with others weekly.

- Familial goals
    1. Actively participate with my children on special days and weekends.

2. Communicate with my immediate family weekly.
3. Develop and live my budget this year.
4. Begin asking for help immediately when needed.
5. Finish school this year.
6. Keep looking for a life partner weekly.

- Physical goals
  1. Exercise daily.
  2. Cook/eat good food daily.
  3. Plan adventurous activities monthly.

- Societal goals
  1. Explore my career options weekly.
  2. Attend more social activities monthly.
  3. Meet more people/make more friends monthly.

Here is a sample Activity List for the Goal List:

- Spiritual activities
  1a. Attend church on Sundays without kids.
  1b. Decide on a church home.
  1c. Bring kids to church.
  2a. Take Sunday evenings to rest and find peace.
  3a. Read each night before going to sleep.
  4a. Talk with others about their beliefs and church weekly.

- Familial activities
  1a. Spend each kid weekend/holiday/vacation doing kid stuff.
  2a. Set aside time each week calling/E-mailing/writing family and friends.
  3a. Set aside time each week to pay bills and work on my budget.
  4a. Monitor my feelings weekly.
  4b. Ask for advice or help from family and friends when needed.

    5a. Invest 8 hours weekly on work toward my college degree.

    6a. Date 3 to 4 times per month.

- Physical activities
  - 1a. Sign up for weekly yoga class.
  - 1b. Do daily stretching.
  - 2a. Shop at the Farmers Market weekly.
  - 2b. Use my healthy cookbooks.
  - 2c. Read *Jane Brody's Guide to Nutrition*.

- Societal activities
  - 1a. Read the *San Francisco Chronicle*/web news for industry information.
  - 1b. Research Life Mapping project weekly.
  - 2a. Host a dinner party at my house next month.
  - 3a. Play in 3-dart tournaments per month, join a league.
  - 3b. Find info on a single parents group.

Lists Are Good

"When the adrenaline is running you forget things, so, you need to have checklists!"cautions Admiral Bidcoff.[6] The admiral has identified a very important organizational concept. Routines, habits, are formed through repetitive action. Unfortunately, until activities have become habits, and sometimes even after they have become habits, we need checklists to make sure we are accomplishing everything we set out to. That is when you decide which of the activities on your list are repetitive. If you only have to do the activity one time, don't worry about establishing a habit. However, if you will be doing it hundreds of times over your lifetime, take the time to think it through. Write down the steps involved. When you think you have optimized the activity, make it a habit! Do it by using your checklist every time you do the activity, until you can do it perfectly without looking at the list. Keep the list, you might need a refresher next year.

Think of it as your form of baseball's spring training. It is very interesting to think that professional baseball players, the best in the world at their game, get together for two months to practice the fundamentals before each season starts. We should do no less. After all, isn't becoming the person you want to be as important as a baseball season?

What About Failure?

What activities will be required to reach your goals? Some of them will be uncomfortable. You can't stay in the same rut and still expect to reach new goals. Becoming uncomfortable is part of the solution; so is failing. You have to fail to learn; you have to fail to have the opportunity to succeed. Babe Ruth hit 714 home runs; he struck out 1,330 times. The Babe's experience gives new meaning to failing: Don't be afraid to fail! "The glory is not in never failing, but in rising every time you fail," states a Chinese proverb. Every failure can make you stronger, as long as you don't give up. Your failures make each success that much more rewarding.

Some people want results without effort. Life doesn't work that way. If something comes too easily, it usually goes just as easily. These people remind me of the story of the chimp who puts his hand into a candy jar. He fills his hand with candy, only to find that he is unable to get the candy out of the jar because his hand is now larger than the opening of the jar. He never lets go of the candy and consequently never tastes it. All he had to do was make a minor correction in his thinking and he would be able to eat all of the candy, one piece at a time. The people unwilling to put in the effort necessary to fulfill their dreams suffer from the same malady.

Patience and Faith

A farmer doesn't plant a crop on a Wednesday expecting to harvest the next day. The farmer prepares the ground, plants the crop, and waters and fertilizes when necessary. All the while, the farmer has faith that months later there will be a crop to harvest. You are preparing the ground by completing your Life Map. The activities you do over the next few months are the planting, watering, and fertilizing. They will produce results, if you have the faith of a farmer. Just as the farmer wouldn't forget to water the fields, even though they show no sign of growth; you shouldn't forget to do those activities you have determined are necessary for the accomplishment of your goals, even if there are no visible signs of progress. One day you will find yourself in the middle of the successes you have dreamed of your whole life.

Budgeting

Money will not bring you happiness. However, mismanagement of money will bring you pressures that can affect your happiness. Therefore, you need to live within a budget. Your career will provide an income. Careful planning will allow you to give to those less fortunate, save for retirement, and still pay your current bills. Without a budget, no amount of income will be enough. You will continue to find new ways to outspend your increased income. The budgeting process begins with an accurate accounting of your take-home income. Find a way to have your withholding taxes come as close to your final tax bill as possible. You should not have a large refund, or owe money, on April 15.

Ten percent of your net income should go into some kind of retirement account and another 10 percent should go to those less fortunate. A third 10 percent should go to reduce your outstanding debt, credit cards, or lines of credit. You should not charge anything until all of your debt is paid off. Once all your debt is paid, charge only what you can pay off completely each month out of the 70 percent you will use to pay your monthly bills. When all of your debt is paid, you should now begin using that 10 percent to build a reserve fund, savings account, or money market account that equals six months of your net income. When the reserve fund is built, this same 10 percent should begin building a long-term-goal fund. A long-term-goal fund is what you use to pay for things like a new car, a down payment on a home, or the kids' college. Remember, this leaves you with the remaining 70 percent to pay those monthly bills. Sure, there are emergencies, but buying a new suit or shoes is not an emergency. Paying for repairs to your car, because your brakes went out, is an emergency. Now, take that 70 percent and decide how you will spend it each month. Remember, that is all there is to spend! There are sample budgets in Appendix B at the end of this book.

The budgeting process is a wonderful way to introduce your children to the fine art of money management. My wife Gail and I began having weekly family council meetings when our children were ages six and eight. The meetings covered a variety of topics: for example, happy things that had happened the prior week, presenting an award to someone in the family who did something special the past week, new problems that came up during the week that needed to be solved, a fun family activity for the day, and of course, budgeting. Each child had his and her own checking account; Gail and I were the bank.

When Gail took the kids to the grocery store and they wanted her to buy them a toy or some candy, she simply asked them if they had enough money in the bank and whether they really wanted to spend it now. If they said they did, they wrote out a check and took the item home. If they didn't have enough money, they weren't able to make that purchase and they learned a valuable lesson, and Gail was saved from a battle over the item. They were continually making their own decisions and learning that they would have to live with that decision. Each week at the meeting, they received their allowance. The first thing they did was decide how much they wanted to save, for college and their first car.

Looking back on it, we should have included a donation to a charity, but at the time we weren't giving that much ourselves—a regret that we are correcting. The children learned some wonderful lessons and acquired some important basic skills: decision making, money management, conflict resolution, selecting and organizing fun activities, participating in and running meetings, and appreciating the wonderful things that happened each week, and the special things other family members did for them.

This was the second most important habit we established in the raising of our children. The most important was to provide a consistent and united image of ourselves as parents. We never disagreed in front of the children on decisions involving them. Therefore, they always knew where they stood and that they could not use one of us against the other. If one of them asked me if they could do something, I would inquire if they had asked their mother. If they had, I would agree with her decision. If for some reason I disagreed with her decision, Gail and I would talk about it privately. We would not change that decision, but we came to an agreement on a united answer for the next time we faced a similar situation. If they hadn't asked Gail, I would give my opinion but would couch it with "Go see if it is okay with your mother." I am proud to say that our children, now fifteen and seventeen, are a constant joy to both of us.

Hail the Doer

Theodore Roosevelt once said:

> It is not the critic who counts; not the man who points out how the strong man stumbles, or where the doer of deeds could have done better. The credit belongs

to the man who is actually in the arena; whose face is marred by dust and sweat and blood; who strives valiantly; who errs and comes short again and again; who knows the great enthusiasms, the great devotions and spends himself in a worthy cause; who at the best knows in the end the triumph of high achievement; and who at the worst, if he fails, at least fails while daring greatly; so that his place shall never be with those cold and timid souls who know neither victory nor defeat.[7]

Dare to do great things! You will never regret the effort!

As you view your Activity List, think of the transitions you will be making as part of a lifelong path of personal learning and self-discovery. Enjoy the activities and the positive changes they will make in your life.

Your Activity List

Spiritual

1. _____
2. _____
3. _____
4. _____

Physical

1. _____
2. _____
3. _____
4. _____

Familial

1. _____
2. _____
3. _____
4. _____

Societal

1. _____
2. _____
3. _____
4. _____

SCHEDULES

DEVELOPING A SCHEDULE is not time management in the traditional sense. It is more akin to putting a puzzle together. You have the pieces, your activities, and you begin to put them together to form a picture, the picture of your ideal week. Most people's picture of their ideal week is chaos. The fear of looking at that chaotic picture has kept them from actually writing down an ideal weekly schedule. They are missing one of the most powerful messages ever known. It has been repeated numerous times over the past twenty-five hundred years. When your actions are in alignment with your inner blueprint, you will find an inner peace that cannot be attained any other way. This feeling comes from being in total control of your life. You are no longer fighting yourself. You no longer need to fight with others. It is a beautiful picture that will bring admiration from all who witness it.

Getting Started

We will begin with the blank schedule on page 90. The first decision you need to make is the time you will get up each morning and the time you will retire each night. Consider the number of hours you need to sleep and still have the energy to reach your goals. It is very difficult to force yourself to perform all your activities, even those you know you want and need to do, when you are tired. Even if you can do it in the short run, eventually it will catch up to you and you will get sick or give up on your schedule altogether. Now, if you are sure you will get enough sleep, put those times in the left-hand column, the time column, at the top and bottom of the schedule. The time column can have any interval you feel is appropriate. Some people use fifteen-minute intervals, some thirty-minute, and some one-hour.

Next, put in the events that you have no control over. Driving the kids to school at 8:00 A.M. or eating dinner at 7:00 P.M. This is usually where people begin to feel claustrophobic. Think about what you are feeling. Understand why you are feeling this way.

Think back to the last time you used a road map. You selected that map because it helped you decide on a route, one that was most pleasing to *you*. That route helped you reach *your* destination. How restricting was that? You used a map—some would not want to be so restricted. You decided on a route— what happened to spontaneity? You reached your destination— but wasn't it forced? Can you see the parallels between this schedule and that map? Your schedule is the itinerary *you* have created for your life. When you complete a week on the schedule, you will understand the freedom it brings. The relief from the stress brought about by others trying to *influence* your activities. The satisfaction in reaching the goals *you* have established, and the happiness you receive because you followed the route that brought you enjoyment and pleasure while achieving your goals, will be more than enough reward for your efforts.

Freedom at Last

This is a good time to discuss the use of the schedule. It is not a prison you are trapped in; it is your guide on life's trail. It is a way to integrate your plan into your life. You are to use it to help you make the best choices each day. You should not expect to ever have an ideal week. Probably not even an ideal

ACTIVITY SCHEDULE

Time	Monday	Tuesday	Wednesday	Thursday	Friday	Saturday	Sunday

day. It is only a tool. Maybe it will help you feel less confine
Also remember that it is a living schedule and you need to keep
changing it to fit your current needs.

Now back to completing the schedule. The next activity you
need to put in your schedule is something you probably don't
have on your Activity List, time for planning and reviewing.
You should identify the first, and/or the last, fifteen to thirty
minutes of each day for reviewing your last day and planning
the next. That is the time when you see how closely you adhered
to your schedule. Anything left undone can be added to the next
day's scheduled events. This is how we keep on schedule. We
are reminded, daily, that we have planned and scheduled activities that need to be done that day. Without this planning and
reviewing time you will not be able to follow any schedule. Time
and other people will separate you from your goals and the activities that lead to their achievement.

During your reviewing time you should ask yourself some
questions. Was my behavior in line with my Principle List yesterday? Did I correctly prioritize my activities yesterday? Did I
do the things that really matter most? Could I have done anything any better? Once a week you should invest ten or fifteen
minutes to look at the whole week. That gives you an overview
of your progress on a scale that is small enough to make the
necessary adjustments while they are still small adjustments.
The time you take to plan and reflect on your week will increase
your confidence, clarify your activities, and reinforce your Goal
List, reducing the likelihood of your becoming overwhelmed.
You will discover important things about yourself and find your
untapped potential. Time set aside for planning and reviewing
will also allow you to unwind and restore your vital resources.
Keep reflecting on balance and harmonize your activities.

Time Management Has Its Place

We can't ignore time management, if we plan on improving
our lives. There are some time management techniques that will

th those extra hours we need to accomplish our
 must understand that everyone has the same 168
ek to accomplish their goals. If we spend them
e won't have any time left to work on our goals.
 our day should be filled by an activity. We will
tivities. If we misuse this freedom, we will waste
our lives. If we are to start our career activities at 9:00 A.M. and
we are still in bed, how can we be successful?

How would you feel if you went to your dental appointment at 9:00 A.M. and they told you that the dentist was still in
bed? What would you do if they asked you to take a seat in the
waiting room and that you would be the third patient he saw
when he arrived? What would you think of that dentist? How
well did he prioritize his activities? Time management is nothing more than getting your priorities straight and doing the supporting activities in a timely manner.

By the way, you are way ahead of most people, since you
have identified your priority activities. Most people are still
thinking about their chaotic lives. Practicing time-saving techniques will free up the time you need to not only complete your
current Activity List, but to allow you to add additional goals
from your Goal List.

Now, let's go over the key elements of time management.

- Don't waste time trying to change things you have no
  control over. Accept them, adapt to them, and move on.
- Keep in touch with reality. Don't waste time in activities
  that disconnect you from reality; daydreaming, drugs,
  TV, etc. An occasional recreation is good for you, but not
  chronic use or abuse; they are self-defeating.
- Repeat activities that increase your self-esteem and avoid
  those that reduce it. How do you feel about yourself after
  you do an activity? If you feel good about yourself, it
  increased your self-esteem. You are not looking for the
  amount of fun associated with an activity. What you are
  looking for here is whether the activity is a positive factor
  in the development of your self-esteem. You are in con-

trol; don't blame others or circumstances for activities that lower your self-esteem. Change them!

- Use your Life Map, your guide, daily. The farther you get from your guide, the greater the possibility your environment or other people will get you off track. Ultimately, you could get lost.
- Maintain the planning and reviewing habit. Every minute you invest in planning and reviewing will return from three to thirty minutes back in future time saved. Planning and reviewing builds upon itself and you will keep getting better and better, thus increasing the time returned for the time invested.
- We need to learn to manage those things that present themselves as urgent. Most urgent activities, and they will pop up every day, should not immediately replace the planned priority activity currently scheduled. We need to learn to minimize those interruptions. Have your calls screened at work and return them during a time reserved for that activity. Learn to leave complete messages and ask that others do the same. This will minimize telephone tag. Use E-mail whenever possible.
- Use a single calendar system. Avoid duplicating entries. The physical tool you will need to maintain your schedule should be small enough for you to carry wherever you go. It should include an area for each day of the year, as well as sections for your phone list and any other lists you feel you need. I prefer the Day-Timer system. You can order a catalog or the product itself by calling 800–225–5005. To maximize your results with this system, I would recommend that you obtain a copy of Charles R. Hobbs's audiocassette tape set *Your Time and Your Life*. You can obtain it from the Nightingale-Conant Corporation by calling 800–323–5552. I don't usually endorse products; however, these two have made a major difference in my gaining control over my use of time.
- Organize your work area. Everything you use regularly should be within your reach, without leaving your chair.

- The next activity you should add to your Life Map represents one of the most dynamic concepts in time management. You should find a place in your schedule for organizational time. Two hours a week will be more than adequate for most people. During this time, you will develop shortcuts that will save you many more hours throughout the rest of your life. What kinds of shortcuts? you ask. For example, maintaining a current phone list and carrying a copy with you at all times. That sounds simple enough, but how is it going to save you time? The activity might take two hours initially and an additional hour annually, but it will save you approximately ten hours annually. That means you have just acquired an additional seven hours the first year and nine hours every year thereafter. Keep an ongoing list with you of activities that are repetitive, like using a computer program to record your expenses. At the end of the year the computer will total your expenses in various categories and even allow you to download the information into a tax program that will do your taxes for you. A big time-saver! During your organizational time each week, look at the list and decide which activity would produce the biggest savings in time, energy, and/or a reduction in frustration. That is the one you need to work on next.
- One of those other lists you should consider is a "grass catcher list," that is, a list is for all of the things you need to do that are not time sensitive. Like picking up the clothes from the cleaners or a spare bottle of contact solution. Then when you find yourself near the cleaners or with time to spare, you can pull out your list and accomplish something. Of course, it is always a good idea to have in your briefcase or purse an interesting book for those very same moments.
- Take 100 percent responsibility in all communications. In conversations, repeat important information using different wording or ask the other person to repeat it to you, so that you may make sure that *you* properly communicated it. That is another big time-saver as it reduces duplicate activi-

ties and the possibility of the severe consequences that sometimes follows miscommunications.

Occasionally We Need a Break

One important point to remember: Whenever you are feeling overwhelmed or overscheduled, take a break and look at your week. If you need to adjust the schedule, do it. If, however, it is a temporary event that has caused the discomfort, keep your schedule and adjust that one week. Some people let this event cause them to give up on planning and scheduling. A big mistake. Just think about the beautiful picture you have created and don't let anyone or anything destroy it.

Another activity you should include in your planning time is a review of your goals. Read your list, then close your eyes and think about the goals. Do not think about the activities. These minireviews will lead to future changes in your Activity List. Whenever you find some free time during the day, take that opportunity to enjoy a minireview. The more you do this activity, the sooner you will reach your goals. The mind is always working on solutions, even when we are enjoying a break.

Now you are ready to add the activities from your Activity List. Think of the puzzle example: Where would each of these activities best fit in your ideal week. Take your time and think about potential conflicts you might be creating. Take your biological clock into consideration. Schedule your most important or strenuous work during the time of the day that you are most alert. Your schedule needs to be compatible with your spouse's and children's ideal schedules. Make sure to leave enough time between activities as well as enough for the activity itself. You will move pieces of the puzzle around many times before you actually settle into a comfortable ideal weekly schedule. There is no need to hurry through this period of your Life Mapping process; your schedule will continually change for the rest of your life. Be flexible enough to recognize the need to change and be proactive enough to actually change. Keep stepping back and looking at the whole picture. Keep asking yourself, "Am I really happy with my ideal week?"

Once you set your foot upon this path, you will continually improve the schedule system you are developing. It is much easier to strike out on a new trail when you have a guide to follow. Outside influences will no longer negatively affect your daily behavior.

Now, you are ready to begin putting the pieces of the puzzle together. Good luck!

A DIFFERENT VIEW OF THE LIFE MAP

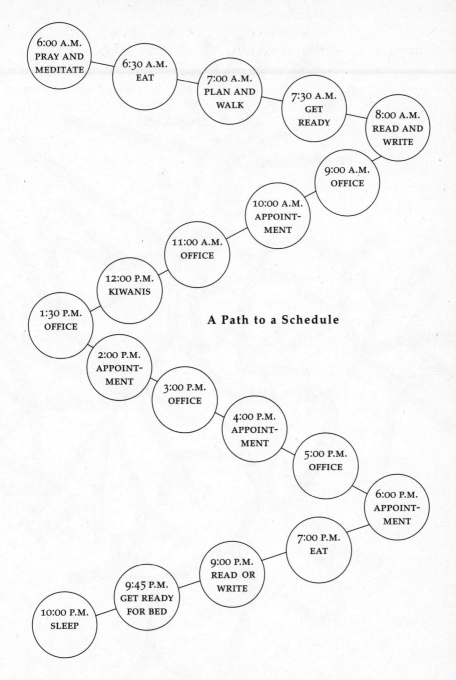

A Path to a Schedule

CREATE YOUR OWN VISION OF A SCHEDULE

How To

So you don't know how you will ever find the time to start this process. No problem! You can attack it in a number of different ways. I would recommend that you pretend you are off to boot camp, preparing for the war of a lifetime, and that you give up all activities that are not mandatory for the next few weeks. Of course, you should go to work, unless you have some unused vacation time. Some of the things you can give up include: TV, reading the newspaper or magazines, answering the phone (turn on your answering machine to cut down on interruptions), socializing (tell your friends you can't see them for a few weeks), cleaning (cut it to a minimum), food (eat less complicated meals), personal accounting (put as many of your bills as possible on automatic payment), civic or volunteer commitments. You can also get up a little earlier or stay up a little later.

Using the time productively is important. Find a quiet space where you are not likely to be interrupted. Remember, this is just for a few weeks. It will be well worth the effort and your family, friends, and that civic organization will appreciate the positive changes it will have in your life. One of the goals of this boot camp experience should be to look for ways to accomplish your goals while keeping your life as simple as possible. Simple means not scheduling unnecessary activities and looking for less complicated solutions to doing those necessary activities.

Downshifting

I just read an article in my monthly Kiwanis magazine by Samuel Greengard, titled, "The Upshot of 'Downshifting.' " Mr. Greengard describes a relatively new trend, "downshifting," which the Trends Research Institute in Rhinebeck, New York, calls one of the hottest movements of the 1990s. A November 1995 issue of *U.S. News & World Report* is quoted as estimating that some 4 percent of all baby boomers have already taken to downshifting—a figure that could rise to 15 percent by the year 2000. So, what is downshifting? It is the dumping of that high-paying, overly stressful job for a simpler, more balanced, and more fulfilling life. Sound familiar? Mr. Greengard warns, "Psychological issues also can take a toll. Those who 'downshift' must suddenly figure out how to structure their day, find their own sense of accomplishment and reward, and use entirely different factors to gauge success." Relax, Mr. Greengard, all downshifters need is a little time to create their Life Map.

Former-CEO-turned-professor William Wilson says, "Instead of investing all of my time and energy to watch a business grow, I now invest in students—and I can often see the direct payoff from all my efforts." Mr. Wilson is earning one-sixth the income he gave up in the corporate world, but he and his wife are enjoying their new, simpler lifestyle. They gave up a thirty-five-hundred-square-foot home in California for a fourteen-hundred-square-foot condo in a Chicago suburb and a less stressful schedule. Sounds like a good trade to me. A trade more of us should seek. With the help of a Life Map, you too could make that trade.

Personal Coaches

You've heard of personal trainers. Now there are personal coaches. They help people keep their lives in shape by coaching them either in person or over the telephone on a regular basis. If you have difficulty developing your Life Map or maintaining your schedule, you might consider hiring a personal coach to assist you.

Make sure the person you hire is certified and has Life Mapping experience. That form of support can be very important during the habit-forming portion of the process. Once your habits are formed, your need for assistance will be lessened. If you use a personal coach to create your original Map, you should consider using the same coach for your first couple of revisions.

The Process

Here is one last review of the process you are about to undertake.

- You will begin by determining your Belief List. The list will grow out of your concept of creation and humanity's purpose.
- Second, you will develop your Principle List, making sure that every principle on the list is supported by one or more of your beliefs. Without that support you will be unable to live by your principles when they are truly tested.
- Third, you will decide on your goals in each of the four areas of life. Keep the balance in your life and the balance will allow you to achieve your maximum potential.
- The fourth step is the dividing of your goals into the activities necessary to achieve them. Continue to break them into smaller and smaller activities, until you can complete each within a week, or preferably a day.
- The fifth and final step is to design an ideal weekly schedule that includes all of the activities on your list. Update it often, and look at it as many times a day as it takes for you to live it.

Goals should be reexamined monthly for the first three to six months. Sometime during those first six months you will switch to quarterly or annual reviews, depending on the number of changes that were needed in the prior period. This process is not about changing who you are every month, quarter, or year. It is about adding depth to the person you are becoming. Like a painter who adds layers of paint over his original sketch, until one day he can step back and look at the masterpiece he has created, you continue to add layers of understanding to your life. Remember, this is a growth experience and your Life Map is the living document that makes it possible. Keep improving it. As you update your Life Map, keep your old copies. They will become a permanent record of your progress.

Frequently Asked Questions

Q.—*Why do you have to have a belief supporting each of your principles?*

A.—Beliefs are the reasons we do things, the *why*. Principles refer to *how* we do things. In the absence of the *why*, we will do only what pleases or benefits us. The *how* becomes unimportant without the *why*. Moses believed in the Ten Commandments because God gave them to him. God was the why, the Ten Commandments were the *how*. If you want to follow your principles, your *how*, you must support it with one of your beliefs, your *why*.

Q.—*Should you use the same schedule every week?*

A.—You will probably never have a week that you live exactly according to your Ideal Weekly Schedule. You should continue to use it as a guide until you need to change the activities currently on the schedule or you feel a need to change times or the order of activities. Few people will use the same schedule for more than a few months. As we evolve, our goals will change and so will the activities required to reach them. You must keep your schedule current. Remember, this is a tool to help you complete the activities that are required to reach your goals. Your schedule will increase the odds of your reaching your goals and speed the process. You are the master, not the schedule. Update it often!

Q.—*What do you do about activities that you were unable to complete?*

A.—Each day during your reviewing and planning time, you should identify unfinished activities and, if possible, complete them within the next few days. Sometimes that is not possible. If the activity was date or time sensitive, a concert, for example, and you missed it, forget about it. Plan to go to the next one.

Q.—*How detailed should I make my Activity List for a particular goal?*

A.—You should continue to break the goal down into smaller and smaller parts, individual activities, until each of the activities can be completed within a week, or preferably a day. Your test question should be "Can I complete this activity this week?" If the answer is no, you need to continue to break it into smaller activities.

Q.—*How do I know what I really believe?*

A.—Your true belief system will evolve from your concept of how it all began and your purpose. You cannot shortcut this process. If you do, you will end up with a belief system in name only and it will not be able to support your Principle List. Take the time to decide what you really believe about how it all began. Then make sure you use a logical thought process to determine your purpose for being here. When Henry Ford developed the gasoline-powered automobile in 1893, he created something that was wholly new. His purpose was to offer an alternative to the horse that would one day make long-distance travel possible for the masses and that would be affordable to the average person. How were you created? Why? What is your purpose for being here? Your belief system is the natural result of the answers to these questions.

Q.—*How old is the Life Mapping process?*

A.—Life Mapping, as described in this book, is sixteen years old. It has evolved from teachings that are thousands of years old. Fads come and go, but wisdom is ageless. Socrates taught his students, "The unexamined life is not worth living." Until you really know yourself, you will feel incomplete, you will be plagued by conflict, and you will never feel true happiness.

Q.—*I can just see myself checking my schedule every half hour to see what's next. Does the schedule ever become second nature?*

A.—Within a few weeks the schedule will become a habit. You will review it at least once per day during your reviewing and planning time. It will need to be updated as activities are completed, goals are fulfilled, and new ones are added, but you will not be looking at it every half hour.

Q.—*I just got sidetracked from my schedule because of unforeseen circumstances. What do I do with the activities that I don't complete for the day?*

A.—If they still need to be done, reschedule them for the following day. Some activities, such as praying, walking, or attending church, will not need to be rescheduled. You just forget about them and try not to miss them tomorrow.

Q.—*Do I use the same schedule week after week?*

A.—You use the same schedule week after week, substituting new activities and goals for those completed, unless the new ones require a schedule modification. You might have to change your schedule to account for changes in activities that you have no control over. As an example, your company changed your hours and you have to be at the office at eight instead of nine.

Q.—*Life Mapping seems like it would be hard to employ without the help of family members. How do I maintain my Map when my family members are not using a Life Map?*

A.—You share your Map with them and work at the necessary conflicts as you would at activities you have no control over.

Q.—*A friend drops by, the phone won't stop ringing, there's a traffic jam, my kid needs help with homework—these events will inevitably happen. How can I possibly plan for them in my schedule?*

A.—You cannot plan for these unforeseen events. You deal with them as they come up and make the necessary adjustments in your schedule, if possible, for the interrupted activities. Remember, your schedule is the ideal and you will probably never live a perfect day, much less a perfect week.

Q.—*I can see myself doing the scheduling for a couple of weeks, and then losing steam. Any tips on how to keep at it?*

A.—Post your Map in as many prominent places as possible. Give copies to as many of your family members, friends, and co-workers as you can, asking them to remind you if they see you off schedule. If you find yourself less motivated, take out those paragraphs you wrote describing your goals and reread them. Get that feeling back. Once you stick with the process for three or four weeks, most of the schedule will have already become habit.

Ask for Help

Make copies of your Life Map and put them everywhere. Start by putting them in places where you are sure to see them daily—on your bathroom mirror, your daily planner, etc. Sharing yourself with your friends is an important part of Life Mapping. When your Map is complete, you should give a copy of it to as many of your friends and family as possible. Your first instinct will be to keep it a secret. You might think you should wait until you are living it before you tell anyone about it. Wrong! You need all the help you can get.

Coach Ben Parks is a man who coached football and wrestling for almost forty years at Menlo-Atherton High School in northern California. He has served as a trainer for the San Francisco 49ers for nearly twenty-five years, training athletes like Jerry Rice, Joe Montana, Roger Craig, and Ronnie Lott. He volunteers many hours serving the boys and girls in our community. He is a great role model who demonstrates his devotion to self-improvement through discipline, training, and a higher set of values. Coach Parks says, "I like to be called a role model, because once you have that pressure, you're inclined to live that way."[1] Another reason to have a Life Map and to share with others.

Coach Parks is one of my community's local heroes. He makes the important point that "once you have the pressure"— provided by other people thinking of you as the person you want to be—"you're inclined to live that way." However, people can't help you if they don't know what you are trying to do. To be sure, opening yourself to other people in this way involves some risk, but you will find that these people love you and want to help you. They are on your side. They want you to be happy. Many of the problems we have with these people stem from their inability to help us. When you show them your Map, you also need to tell them what you expect from them.

You should expect kindly reminders when your behavior is in conflict with your stated principles or activities. Some people will use a single word, like "helping," or a hand signal, like one finger pointing to the sky. When you hear or see the signal, you immediately know you need to correct your behavior. Did you give that person control over you? No! You gave that person the permission to help you gain control over yourself. The final decision will always be yours. You will be very surprised at how willing and encouraging these people will be. You should offer to return the favor if there is any area in which they feel they need help. Remember, you are forming a team to help you create the positive habits that will lead you to your nobler part.

The stronger you become, the more you will have to share with others. Sharing will speed your development. As much as you try to give to others, you will find that more keeps coming back to you. That is one of the natural laws: The more you truly give of yourself, the greater you become and the more you are able to give. According to Alexandra Stoddard, "Friendship is the highest degree of perfection in society."[2] Let others help you and help as many of them as you can.

Are You Dead?

On April 9, 1995, Bill Cosby gave a lecture at Howard University on "Contributing to Society." That lecture was aired on C-SPAN. The lecture's title really should have been "Are You Dead?" He was addressing the students and faculty of the university. Throughout the lecture he pointed to unconscious behaviors that are detrimental to our society and followed each example by asking, "Are you dead?" He referred to the people who exhibited these behaviors as "dead people." His definition of a "dead person" was someone who has given up on him- or herself. Someone who is just accepting life as it comes: They buy albums that debase society. They go to movies that promote random sex and graphic violence. They are twelve-year-old girls who have so little respect for themselves that they go out and get pregnant. They are crack dealers who peddle death to support their own habits. They are fifth-generation residents of the projects.

Have you given up on yourself? Do you buy albums or go to movies that are sending us negative images? Are you making up excuses for your failures or deviant behavior? Do you show the proper respect for your elders, for younger people, and for yourself?

You know when you do something wrong. Get on with your life and quit making excuses. Do the best you can at whatever you try; don't settle for being a professional "C" student or person. Make sure you are leaving something for those who will follow you. Go out into the community and find as many "dead people" as you can and help them. Disassociate yourself from stereotyping. You want people to accept you as an individual; so why would you lump others into groups?

Do you have a problem with parenting? You need to teach your children right from wrong; that is what being a parent is all about. You have to discuss your children's problems because they won't be solved by shaking a finger at them.

You are hungry for truth, honesty, and fairness in your life.

So don't settle for half-truths from your leaders. Don't be afraid to demand what is right, for yourself and for others. You can be one of the world's heroes. But it won't happen by itself. You have to make an honest effort to make a difference. This is Bill Cosby's version of Life Mapping.

"If a man happens to find himself, he has a mansion which he can inhabit with dignity all the days of his life," said the great American writer James Michener.[3] In the process of finding yourself, remember to try to enjoy each moment. "Stay in the moment and make each day your masterpiece," as John Wooden said in an interview in the *San Francisco Chronicle*.[4] John Wooden is an example of a man living his map. He has created his masterpiece! Will you create yours?

Don't Let Yourself Down!

I hope you will complete your life without regrets. When I pass into the next lifetime, I will not be compared with Moses, Buddha, or Jesus. I will be compared with the person I was capable of becoming. I will not let myself down! "Let him that would move the world, first move himself," said Socrates.

This reminds me of a poem by Edgar A. Guest:

Compensation

I'd like to think when life is done
    That I had filled a needed post,
That here and there I'd paid my fare
    With more than idle talk and boast;
That I had taken gifts divine,
The breath of life and manhood fine,
And tried to use them now and then
In service for my fellow men.

I'd hate to think when life is through
    That I had lived my round of years
A useless kind, that leaves behind

No record in this vale of tears;
That I had wasted all my days
By treading only selfish ways,
And that this world would be the same
If it had never known my name.

I'd like to think that here and there,
    When I am gone, there shall remain
A happier spot that might have not
    Existed had I toiled for gain;
That some one's cheery voice and smile
Shall prove that I had been worth while;
That I had paid with something fine
My debt to God for life divine.[5]

How will you know when your map is directing you down the right path? You will know when each day you feel a little calmer, and when your daily behavior and actions come ever closer to representing the person you want to become. And ultimately, when you can ponder your yesterdays without regrets and your tomorrows without fears, then you are on the correct path!

Why should we change? Because we are not yet perfect! As you change and update your Life Map, you may want to reread this book. Be patient; there are no quick fixes. As your life improves and things become clearer, your understanding of this material will deepen. You will see and understand things you missed in the first reading. The compound effect of multiple readings will astound you.

At the beginning of this book I asked you whether you would act. I also answered that you would if you are ready. I hope you are ready! Each day that passes is another day lost. Begin to seek your nobler part, today! "Seek, and ye shall find" (Matthew 7:7). If you are a seeker, you have found your answer. This is the process that will help you find yourself. Let the musicians make music! The best is yet to be!

DOES IT WORK?

IF YOU ARE WONDERING if you can find meaning, peace, and happiness in this world, you can. If you are wondering if you can raise a happy, healthy family in this world, you can. If you are wondering if you can become a role model to your children and the rest of your community, you can.

Life Mapping works! It has brought peace and happiness to my family. My wife, Gail, our two teenage children, and I live as harmonious a life as you can imagine. We are living examples of the benefits of Life Mapping. Let me share some examples with you.

Gail explains her Life Mapping experience: "Using time management principles alone allowed me to fill my day with activities. At the end of these busy days I still felt like I wasn't able to get enough done. I was volunteering at the children's school and was able to implement a lot of new programs into their school. There was now a new hot lunch program and a new library. There were school board meetings and fund-raisers to plan. But all of this activity was infringing on the time that I used to spend reading to the children. I found myself saying, 'I can't tonight . . .' I was nervous and frustrated but knew there was no time in the day to do more activities.

"The Life Mapping process helped me balance my life; the importance of every activity became more clear. It was after prioritizing activities and balancing the different areas of my life that the problems and solutions became clear. Scheduling time with my family is one of my highest priorities. I've learned to say no more often. Focusing all of my attention on what is truly important in my life gave each activity scheduled a significance it never had before. Now when I'm doing something as simple as playing cards with my father, I'm no longer concerned about other things that I could be doing. This activity was chosen and scheduled because it was the most important thing that I wanted to do, at that time. Now I can totally enjoy the time with him. There is now time to spend talking with Bill, time to visit with Emily when shopping for shoes, and time to laugh with Josh over a game of Scrabble. This balance has relieved much of the pressure in the decision making in my life. It has become easier to say no because I know that I truly do not have time to do everything. Life seems to travel by so quickly that it is important to grab the moments you can to spend with those you love."

Ray, one of the adults currently enrolled in a Life Mapping class, explains what it has meant to him: "Life Mapping has given me some hope to be able to figure out how to achieve my goals. Before I met you, I was struggling with direction in my life. As a single parent, trying to raise two children, it was hard to know how to set an example for the children." Life Mapping is only a tool. As Ray has discovered, it only works if you do.

Raisa, an adult who completed the class two years ago, has continued to update her schedule and finds the commitment to the process motivating. She has gone back to school and regularly involves herself in group activities with other singles. She is living a more fulfilling life and is truly in charge of it.

Teenagers today face a confusing world of peer pressure, mass advertising, and parental expectations, and too often they face this world without the benefit of positive role models. My current class of high school juniors have identified the following benefits to the Life Mapping process. Although their minds are filled with conflicting ideas on creation, purpose, and beliefs, Life Mapping allows them to discuss these concepts in a nonthreatening way. They are able to clear away some of their personal conflicts. They learn that others share their inner feelings. The planning and scheduling of activities teaches them techniques that leverage their time and abilities. The majority of

these students understand the process and benefit from the experience. Most important, they are now better prepared for further exploration and growth.

Remember the *Sierra Club Bulletin* story, "Three Little
Words," discussed in Chapter 3, about the researchers who
asked a preschool class, "Who knows how to sing?" and every
child eagerly responded that they could sing (and dance and
draw). It seems that somewhere between preschool and college
we lose these abilities. How did we lose them?

Some might argue that we never had them, but they would
be wrong. We lost them when we believed we lost them. We
need to believe in ourselves. We need to believe in others. Most
important, we need to believe in the future. Yes, Life Mapping
works. It works because it enables us to see the future. It is a
future we can aspire to seeing actualized. As Ray said, it gives
people the hope that they can achieve their goals!

It begins with an individual, like Ray. It spreads to his children and the people he will eventually mentor. Over time the
community is influenced to set and achieve positive goals. Finally, when there are enough Rays and communities influenced,
the world becomes a kinder place. You and I need to strive to
become like Ray. We need to support the Rays of this world.
They are our future!

A number of people have asked me to explain how Life
Mapping principles helped the insurance district I was managing achieve such phenomenal results. In Chapter 1, I told you
we climbed from 50th to 1st regionally and from 1,150th to 38th
nationally over a nine-year period. To put this achievement into
perspective, we passed a district that had led our region for the
better part of thirty years. That district was highly motivated
by promotions and included a number of agents who regularly
placed in the top fifty nationally. We not only passed them; we
sustained our position for three years. How was that possible?

It begins with a vision that is not ruled by short-term results
or peer pressure. We were not in a hurry to make our mark. We
focused on the long-term results of our decisions. Other districts
stressed workaholic behavior, especially with newly hired
agents. We taught each agent the process that would bring

steadily improving results within a framework of a balanced life. A balanced life meant that we scheduled time each week to spend with our families, in our work, to take care of our bodies, and to have some fun. Our agents were happier with themselves and their careers. Happy people can maintain the processes that produce long-term results. They are not fighting themselves.

An example might help you understand the process. Our company, like many other sales organizations, stresses sales promotions. The months of June and October are designated life insurance promotion months. Special awards and incentives are available to the agents and districts that sell the most life insurance. The problem this creates is a flurry of activity. Much of the insurance written during this time is not quality business. The flurry produces an imbalance in the workload in the office. During the months preceding the promotion, those agents caught up in the game intentionally hold down their production. The months following the promotion they spend recovering from the workload that their offices are ill-prepared to handle. So this results in life insurance written for the wrong reasons and of less than the desired quality. By year's end most of these promotion month heroes and heroines are not among the top agents, who are measured annually on the amount and quality of the life insurance they produce.

Our district did not participate in these promotion months. We didn't boycott them; we just kept producing the quality business that our policyholders needed. When December was drawing to a close, there we were, unnoticed all year and yet somehow mysteriously at the top of the year-end reports. We just did a little every day ... every day ... a little like the tortoise and the hare.

Consistency is the principle of Life Mapping that rewards those who stay the course. Figure out the activities that you need to be doing every day to reach your long-term goals ... then just keep doing them *every day*!

Appendix A

Sample Life Maps

So HOW DOES IT FEEL to have your own Life Map? Empowering, isn't it! May your will guide you to the person you want to be, *the real you*!

Kyla Lyn's Life Map

The Purpose of Life

We are here to discover our purpose, to live it, and to share the process with others.

The Purpose of My Life

My purpose in life is to be a lifelong learner and to share my knowledge with others. It is a process of self-discovery as well as enlightenment.

My Belief List

1. I believe in fate.
2. I do not believe in coincidences.
3. I believe in a higher power.
4. I believe that every individual has a purpose.

5. I believe we are here to contribute something.
6. I believe life is a journey of self-discovery.
7. I believe in peace on earth.
8. I believe in love.
9. I believe in myself.
10. I believe that all people are good.
11. I believe that parenting determines the future.
12. I believe adults can learn from children.
13. I believe in giving more than you receive.
14. I believe that we are responsible for saving the environment.
15. I believe that we need to explore the universe.
16. I believe in intelligent life on other planets.

The Principle List

1. I will treat others fairly. (4) [Numbers refer to numbers on the Belief List.]
2. I will demonstrate loyalty. (10)
3. I will make well-thought-out decisions. (4 and 6)
4. I will be a positive role model for my children. (11)
5. I will be an active listener. (6)
6. I will make mistakes and learn from them. (6)
7. I will be honest with myself and others. (9)
8. I will be grateful for what I have. (13)
9. I will be where I am with focus. (4)
10. I will have discipline in my routine. (4)
11. I will strive to inspire others. (4)
12. I will openly show love and respect for others. (8)
13. I will have an open mind. (6)

My Goals

- Spiritual goals
  1. Find a church this year.
  2. Spend time alone weekly.
  3. Read daily.
  4. Share with others weekly.

- Familial goals
    1. Actively participate with my children on special days and weekends.
    2. Communicate with my immediate family weekly.
    3. Develop and live my budget this year.
    4. Begin asking for help immediately when needed.
    5. Finish school this year.
    6. Keep looking for a life partner weekly.

- Physical goals
    1. Exercise daily.
    2. Cook/eat good food daily.
    3. Plan adventurous activities monthly.

- Societal goals
    1. Explore my career options weekly.
    2. Attend more social activities monthly.
    3. Meet more people/make more friends monthly.

My Activity List

- Spiritual activities
    1a. Attend church on Sundays without kids.
    1b. Decide on a church home.
    1c. Bring kids to church.
    2a. Take Sunday evenings to rest and find peace.
    3a. Read each night before going to sleep.
    4a. Talk with others about their beliefs and church weekly.

- Familial activities
    1a. Spend each kid weekend/holiday/vacation doing kid stuff.
    2a. Set aside time each week for calling/E-mailing/ writing family and friends.
    3a. Set aside time each week to pay bills and work on my budget.
    4a. Monitor my feelings weekly.

4b. Ask for advice or help from family and friends when needed.

5a. Invest 8 hours weekly on University of Phoenix work toward my degree.

6a. Date 3 to 4 times per month.

- Physical activities
  1a. Sign up for weekly yoga class.
  1b. Do daily stretching.
  2a. Shop at the Farmers Market weekly.
  2b. Use my healthy cookbooks.
  2c. Read *Jane Brody's Guide to Nutrition.*

- Societal activities
  1a. Read the *Chronicle*/web news for industry information.
  1b. Research Life Mapping project weekly.
  2a. Host a dinner party at my house next month.
  3a. Play in 3-dart tournaments per month, join a league.
  3b. Find info on a single-parents group.

KYLA LYN'S 1997 SCHEDULE

TIME	MONDAY	TUESDAY	WEDNESDAY	THURSDAY	FRIDAY	SATURDAY	SUNDAY
6:00	stretch/shower	stretch/shower	stretch/shower	stretch/shower	stretch/shower	stretch/shower	stretch/shower
7:00	eat/mail/TV	eat/mail/TV	eat/mail/TV	eat/mail/TV	eat/mail/TV	eat	eat
8:00	work	work	work	work	work	kids	kids
9:00	work	work	work	work	work	market	clean
10:00	work	work	work	work	work	grocery	clean
11:00	work	work	work	work	work	fun	fun
12:00	lunch	lunch	lunch	lunch	lunch	lunch	lunch
1:00	work	work	work	work	work	fun	learn/fun
2:00	work	work	work	work	work	fun	learn/fun
3:00	work	work	work	work	work	fun	learn/fun
4:00	work	work	work	work	work	fun	learn/fun
5:00	work	work	work	work	work	dinner	dinner
6:00	dinner	dinner	dinner	dinner	p/u kids	fun	kids home
7:00	research	school	school	school	dinner	finances	write
8:00	research	school	school	school	kids	laundry	E-mail
9:00	social	school	school	school	kids	read/TV	call
10:00	read/TV	read/TV	read/TV	read/TV	read/TV	read/TV	read/TV
11:00	sleep	sleep	sleep	sleep	sleep	sleep	sleep
12:00	sleep	sleep	sleep	sleep	sleep	sleep	sleep

Benjamin's Life Map

The Purpose of Life

To be fully Human: To feel good about yourself, achieving your goals and happiness. Setting yourself a "good" moral code and respecting it. To evolve in but also with the society.

The Purpose of My Life

To be happy. To set myself goals and to do my best in achieving them without giving up. To do what is good for me. Do for/to the others what I would like people to do for/to me.

My Belief List

1. I think that God is not involved in creation, I believe in the theory of evolution.
2. I believe in being happy.
3. I believe in surviving in our society and if possible to evolve as a better person in our society but also to evolve in a higher social rank.
4. I believe in setting goals and doing your best in achieving them.
5. I believe you should never use violence or harm someone physically.
6. I believe in respecting yourself as well as others because everyone is born equal.
7. I believe in helping the ones in need.

The Principles I Will Live My Life By

1. I will be happy. (2)
2. I will fight my way in our society. (3)
3. I will set myself goals and never give up. (4)
4. I will not use physical violence. (5)

5. I will respect others as well as myself. (6)
6. I will not be a racist or bigot. (6)
7. I will be self-confident and have a high opinion of myself. (6)
8. I will be good and generous to others. (7)

My Goals

- Spiritual goals
    1. Think every day before acting so that I don't commit too many mistakes.

- Familial goals
    1. Stay in touch with my family in France weekly.

- Physical goals
    1. Take care of my body daily. I will not smoke, drink, use drugs, and will set myself a diet based on healthy food.
    2. I will work to stay in shape daily.

- Societal goals
    1. Get good grades in school this year and next for a better future and a better life.
    2. I will do my homework entirely every day.
    3. Ask questions daily if I don't understand.

My Activity List

- Spiritual activities
    1a. Talk and listen to others as much as possible about their morality and their point of view.
    1b. I will set myself a morality set on a good common sense.

- Familial activities
    1a. I will call my family in France at least once a week and fax them.

- Physical activities
    1a. I will set myself a diet based on healthy food.
    1b. I will not eat "junk food" or eat snacks between meals.
    2a. To stay in shape, I will go to basketball practice every day.
    2b. To improve my game, I will do extra practice on the weekends.

- Societal activities
    2a. I will do all my homework, and even extras.
    3a. I will be attentive in class.
    3b. Ask questions if I don't understand.

BEN'S 1997 SCHEDULE

TIME	MONDAY	TUESDAY	WEDNESDAY	THURSDAY	FRIDAY	SATURDAY	SUNDAY
6:50	get up	get up	get up	get up	get up	sleep	sleep
7:00	wash/dress	wash/dress	wash/dress	wash/dress	wash/dress		
7:20	breakfast	breakfast	breakfast	breakfast	breakfast		
7:35	leave for school	leave for school	leave for school	leave for school	leave for school		
8:00	school	school	school	school	school		
10:00	break	break	break	break	break		
11:00						get up	get up
						call France	homework
12:00	lunch	lunch	lunch	lunch	lunch	homework	
1:00						lunch	lunch
2:30	school ends	school ends	school ends	school ends	school ends		
3:00	homework	homework	homework	homework	homework		
5:00	basketball	basketball	basketball	basketball	basketball		
7:00	shower	shower	shower	shower	shower		
7:30	free time	free time	free time	free time	free time		
8:00	dinner	dinner	dinner	dinner	dinner		
8:30	free time	free time	free time	free time	free time		
9:00							
9:30							
10:00							
10:30							
11:00	plan	plan	plan	plan	plan		
11:30	sleep	sleep	sleep	sleep	sleep		

Mark's Life Map

The Purpose of Life

The purpose of life varies from person to person. Sometimes it seems that the purpose of life is to discover the purpose of life. Some people believe that life is created by God. For the people who believe that life is created by God, the purpose of life might be to reach happiness. Happiness, in my opinion, can be reached by trying to enjoy every situation that is faced. For people who reject the notion that life is created by God, the purpose of life might be to survive, or live by the "rule of the jungle." In other words, if we reject the idea that we are created by an intelligent force (such as God), we must believe that our sole purpose on Earth is to pass on our genes to the next generation, and continue the evolutionary process.

The Purpose of My Life

I believe that there is an intelligent unifying force that created all aspects of the Universe, including life. Because of this belief, I believe that the purpose of my life is to definitely find happiness. I believe that I can reach happiness through living up to my full potential, and using the gifts and talents that God gave me to make this World a better place.

My Belief List

1. I believe that a force of reason and intelligence created and controls the Universe.
2. I believe that everything has a *cause*, and that everything has a *consequence*.
3. I believe that humans evolved for a reason, be it for a Scientific reason, or a theological reason, there is a reason. The Scientific explanation for evolution

seems to point in the direction of the argument that organisms must strive to survive. I believe that survival is important, but it is not our sole purpose for existence.

4. I believe that on a Universal level, it is better to do good deeds than evil deeds. Although bad tidings happen to good people sometimes, people should continue to do good deeds. If a person lives a life of goodness, and receives bad tidings, somewhere else in the Universe someone will receive the goodness that is manifested by the truly good person.

5. I believe that the best way to learn a lesson, at times, can be to suffer. Suffering can be a blessing in disguise.

6. I believe that humans are immortal. When our body dies it will go back to nature, where it came from. We will still be as much a part of the Universe when we are dead as when we were alive. Although we may not be able to sense it, when we are dead we are still an integral part of the Universe.

7. I believe that God helps the people who help themselves, as well as others.

My Principle List

1. I will try my best to accomplish any effort. This principle is supported by my belief that every action has a consequence, and I want to receive a positive consequence. (2)

2. I will help other people succeed whenever I can. This is supported by my belief that on a Universal level it is better to do good deeds as opposed to evil deeds. (4)

3. I will not be discouraged by failure, and bad tidings. The principle is supported by my belief that suffering can be the best way to learn a lesson. (5)

4. I will always try my best to improve myself. This principle is supported by my belief that God helps people who help themselves. (7)

My Goals

- Spiritual goals
    1. I will pray before each meal to thank God.
    2. I will pray to thank God whenever I am blessed in any way (as when I accomplish a goal, etc.).
    3. I will pray for the Lord's guidance every time I am faced with a test of my ability.

- Familial goals
    1. I will visit my grandparents at least once a week.
    2. I will take my mother and father out to lunch or dinner once every three months.

- Physical goals
    1. I will do 50 push-ups every day.
    2. I will eat 3 meals daily.

- Societal goals
    1. I will join 3 community service projects before the year ends.

My Activity List

- Spiritual activities
    1a. In order for it to be possible for me to pray before meals, I will arrange for me to bring a Bible to the dinner table, so that I can read a passage for the whole family to reflect on.
    3a. In order to pray for assistance, and in thanksgiving, I will arrange for me to have a silent time each day, so that I can pray to the Lord.

- Physical activities
    1a. In order for me to do 50 push-ups every day, I will find a comfortable place in my room for me to do push-ups.
    2a. In order to eat 3 square meals each day, I will ask my mother to prepare me a 3-course breakfast and dinner every day (lunch is provided by school).

- Familial activities
    1a. In order to visit my grandparents weekly, I will call them up on the telephone and arrange a time to visit their house to eat dinner and talk about life.
    2a. In order to treat my parents to lunch or dinner, I will talk with them so that we can agree on a day, a time, and a place to eat.

- Societal activities
    1a. In order to complete 3 community service projects by the end of the year, I will correspond with Mr. Truddelle, who is in charge of the National Honor Society at school. I belong to the National Honor Society, and Mr. Truddelle will be able to give me advice as to how I should complete my community service projects.

MARK'S 1997 SCHEDULE

TIME	MONDAY	TUESDAY	WEDNESDAY	THURSDAY	FRIDAY	SATURDAY	SUNDAY
6:00	Shower	Shower	Shower	Shower	Shower	Sleep	Sleep
6:30	Breakfast	Breakfast	Breakfast	Breakfast	Breakfast	"	"
7:00	Go to school	Go to school	Go to school	Go to school	Go to school	"	"
7:30							
8:00	School	School	School	School	School		
8:30							
9:00						"	
9:30							"
10:00						"	
10:30						"	Breakfast
11:00						"	Shower
11:30							Clean room
12:00	Lunch	Lunch	Lunch	Lunch	Lunch	Family Activity	Walk w/dad
1:00							
1:30						"	
2:00							Lunch
2:30				.		Lunch	Call grandparents
3:00	Homework	Homework	Homework	Community service	Free time	Free time	Homework
3:30							"
4:00							
4:30							
5:00	Free time	Free time	Yearbook			Visit grandparents	"
5:30					Push-ups		
6:00	Dinner	Dinner			See friends	Dinner	Dinner
6:30	Homework	Homework	Dinner	Collossus		Watch movie	"
7:00			Homework				Television
7:30				Dinner			
8:00				Homework	Dinner	Call girlfriend	Read
8:30					See friends	Read	
9:00	Call girlfriend	Call girlfriend				"	Call girlfriend
9:30	Push-ups	Push-ups				Free time	Push-ups
10:00	Homework	Homework					Sleep
10:30	Relax	Relax	Call girlfriend				"
11:00	Sleep	Sleep	Push-ups		Watch movie	Push-ups	"
11:30			Sleep			Sleep	"
12:00				Push-ups		"	"

Gail's Life Map

The Purpose of Life

To learn how life is to be lived and then to live it.

The Purpose of My Life

My purpose is to live my life with integrity and to make a positive difference in the lives of others.

My Belief List

1. I believe in an all-loving God.
2. I believe that God created man in his image.
3. I believe that God sent his son Jesus to be our guide for our life on earth.
4. I believe that man's highest accomplishment, greatest joy, and widest usefulness is in living in alignment with this example.

My Principle List

1. I will treat others as I would like to be treated. (3)
2. I will stay in condition mentally, morally, and physically. I will nurture a hunger for knowledge. I will read and keep searching for untapped potential. (4)
3. I will be honest and reliable. (3)
4. I will enjoy life and have fun on the journey. (4)
5. I will forgive and not harbor grudges. (3)
6. I will be kindhearted. I will listen attentively and with an open mind. I will think before I speak so that my words will not hurt unnecessarily. (4)
7. I will be thankful. (2)
8. I will maintain a positive attitude. (4)

9. I will trust in God that misfortune and grief help us to grow strong. (1)

My Goals List

- Spiritual goals
    1. Plan daily.
    2. Read weekly.
    3. Write daily.

- Family goals
    1. Continue to develop relationship with Bill daily.
    2. Help Josh and Emily get greater joy in their lives daily.
    3. Spend time with Grandpa daily.
    4. Family council meetings weekly.
    5. Call Mary and Jim twice a month.

- Societal goals
    1. Work with Thear weekly.
    2. Volunteer at schools twice a year.
    3. Help at Kiwanis twice a year.
    4. Lunch with friends weekly.
    5. State Farm reinspections weekly.
    6. Work to renew license annually.
    7. Work on albums weekly.

- Physical goals
    1. Take vitamins daily.
    2. Exercise daily.
    3. Keep weight at 112 and diet healthy daily.

My Activity List

- Spiritual activities
    1a. Plan—20 minutes daily—30 minutes weekly.
    2a. Read—2 hrs. per week.
    3a. Write in journal daily.

- Family activities
    - 1a. Date night once per week.
    - 1b. Plan daily with Bill—20 min.
    - 2a. Take time when they want to talk.
    - 2b. Play games once a week.
    - 2c. Help with homework when asked.
    - 2d. Help them reach their goals.
    - 3a. Cards 4 times a week.
    - 3b. Go to the library once a week.
    - 3c. Work on mail and accounting daily.
    - 4a. Weekly or monthly as needed.
    - 5a. Call Mary and Jim once every two weeks.

- Societal activities
    - 1a. Thear, serve on two committees.
    - 2a. School, work two events.
    - 3a. Kiwanis, work on art festival and tree lot dinner.
    - 4a. Lunch with friends once per week.
    - 5a. Reinspections, do them twice per month plus set up.
    - 6a. Renew license, order tests.
    - 7a. Work on albums, one hour per week.

- Physical activities
    - 1a. Take vitamins daily.
    - 2a. Exercise by walking two miles with Bill and Murphy.
    - 3a. Diet if needed and work on menus weekly.

GAIL'S 1997 SCHEDULE

TIME	MONDAY	TUESDAY	WEDNESDAY	THURSDAY	FRIDAY	SATURDAY	SUNDAY
6:00	Bed	Bed	Bed	Bed	Bed	Bed	Bed
6:30	Breakfast	Breakfast	Breakfast	Breakfast	Breakfast	"	"
7:00	Plan/Walk	Plan/Walk	Plan/Walk	Plan/Walk	Plan/Walk	"	"
7:30	Walk Murphy	Walk Murphy	Walk Murphy	Walk Murphy	Walk Murphy	Plan/Walk	Plan/Walk
8:00	Get ready	Get ready	Get ready	Get ready	Get ready	Walk Murphy	Walk
8:30	"	"	"	"	"	Get ready	Walk Murphy
9:00	Work	Cleaners		Weekly Menu	Work	"	Get Ready
9:30	"	"		"	"	Peapod/ Laundry	"
10:00	"	Laundry	Inspect/Play	Laundry	"	"	Read
10:30	"	"	"	"	"	"	"
11:00	"		"		"	"	Family Council
11:30	"		"		"		"
12:00	Lunch	Lunch w/ Friend	Lunch	Lunch	Lunch	Lunch	Lunch
1:00	Work	"	Inspect/Play	Library	Work	Change Sheets	
1:30	"	Play Cards	"		"	"	
2:00	"	"	"	Play Cards	"	Albums	
2:30	"	Mail	"	"	"	"	
3:00	P/U Emily	P/U Emily	P/U Emily	P/U Emily	P/U Emily		Play Cards
3:30	Mail	Mail	Mail	Mail	Mail	Mail	"
4:00							
4:30	Make Dinner	Make Dinner	Make Dinner	Make Dinner	Make Dinner	Make Dinner	Make Dinner
5:00	"	"	"	"	"	"	'
5:30	Dinner	Dinner	Dinner	Dinner	Dinner	Dinner	Dinner
6:00	Do Dishes	Do Dishes	Do Dishes	Do Dishes	Do Dishes	Do Dishes	Do Dishes
6:30	"	"	"	"	Date Night	"	"
7:00	Play Cards	Meetings for Thear	Meetings for School		"		
7:30	"	"	"		"	Ask to Play Game	
8:00		"	"		"	"	
8:30	Call Jim/Mary	"	"	Order Groceries	"	"	
9:00	"	Read/Write	Read/Write	Pay Bills	"	"	Pay Bills
9:30	Write	Write	Write	Write	"	Write	Review Week
10:00	Bed	Bed	Bed	Bed	"	Bed	Bed
10:30	"	"	"	"	"	"	"
11:00	"	"	"	"	Write	"	"
11:30	"	"	"	"	Bed	"	"
12:00	"	"	"	"	"	"	"

Richard's Life Map

The Purpose of Life

We are here to demonstrate, through free agency, that we desire to and are worthy of returning to our Lord in heaven.

The Purpose of My Life

My purpose is to learn right from wrong and to be an example for others.

My Belief List

1. I believe in Jesus Christ, the Father, and the Holy Spirit.
2. I believe in the promises the Lord has given us.
3. I believe in eternal life after death with the Holy Father if we repent of our sins and we obey the Ten Commandments and the Word of Wisdom.
4. I believe in the Holy Bible and the Book of Mormon.
5. I believe in the 10 Commandments and The Word of Wisdom because I have experienced life without these spiritual guidelines (rules).
6. I believe that through the Holy Ghost I will know what is true if I treat my body as a temple.
7. I believe in myself and that whatever I put my mind to, I can achieve with the help of the Lord.
8. I believe that the Lord has given each one of us free agency to choose right from wrong, and from these experiences we form our character.
9. I believe that I am in control of my mind, thoughts, and actions; and the only thing I can't control are natural occurrences, and other people because

they have also been given free agency from the
Lord to determine their future.

10. I believe that the world revolves around searching
and expressing one's love for one another.

11. I believe that the ultimate form of love which we
are to learn from was demonstrated through
Jesus Christ while performing unconditional acts
of love through charity.

12. I believe we all have God-given talents which need
to be found, strengthened, and shared with other
human beings.

13. I believe in doing unto others as you would have
done unto you.

14. I believe that the Lord has given us free agency
to choose whether we will return to him in
heaven.

15. I believe we must learn from our experiences in
trying to follow in Jesus' footsteps (who was the
only perfect human example) so that we may be
more like him as time goes on.

16. I believe that love will fill emptiness, overcome
struggles, and unite us together, and ultimately
with our Father in heaven.

17. I believe that not until I love myself, can I love
another.

18. I believe that when I have my priorities in line
(beginning with spiritual goals), everything else
will fall into place.

19. I believe that the major obstacle preventing us from
returning to our heavenly Father's love is the
discouragement which the Devil continues to
make us feel. (ex. "I'm not good enough to . . ."
or "I have to make myself better (perfect) before
I return to the Lord.")

20. I believe that the Lord will forgive us of most of
our sins if we repent with a sincere heart and
have faith in him.

The Principle List

1. *Love*—I will love others as much as the Lord and myself. (16)
2. *Integrity*—I will live with integrity, especially when most unpopular. (4, 13)
3. *Patience*—I will live with patience no matter how urgent or frustrated I become and realize that timing plays an important role. (2)
4. *Honesty*—I will be honest in all my doings. (13)
5. *Judgment*—I will not judge others for their wrongdoings and leave that to the Lord. (5, 9, 13)
6. *Understanding*—(Listening) I will seek to understand before being understood. (4)
7. *Action*—I will take immediate action upon my decisions. (7)
8. *Persistence*—I will persist in my goals and alter my approaches when needed. (7, 19)
9. *Analytical*—I will analyze things from A to Z and look at the possible repercussions of my decisions. (8)
10. *Listen*—I will listen intently. (13)
11. *Optimistic*—I will be optimistic. (2, 3, 17)
12. *Carpe Diem*—I will seize the day for I am exchanging a day of my life for it and I will never get it back. (15)
13. *Habits*—I will be a slave to my good habits; and alter my habits which are bad. (5, 9)
14. *Learn*—I will learn from my experiences. (4, 6, 15)
15. *Teachable*—I will be open-minded and teachable in new ideas (concepts) of importance, realizing that we will never know everything. (4, 15)
16. *Chastity*—I will remain chaste until marriage. (5)
17. *Believe*—I will believe in myself, others, and especially in the Lord. (1, 4, 5)
18. *Obedient*—I will follow the Ten Commandments

and the Word of Wisdom (not smoke, drink
alcohol, and coffee or tea). (5)

19. *Addiction*—I will avoid things which I may become
    addicted to in a harmful way. (5)

20. *Temple*—I will treat my body like a temple.
    (5, 6, 14)

21. *Humble*—I will be humble at times of success and
    in all doings. (13, 19, 20)

22. *Grateful*—I will be grateful for what God has given
    me temporally and spiritually and for the
    experiences he has allowed me. (2, 4)

23. *Commit*—I shall commit to my words, and goals and
    alter them only after having given it 110%. (7)

24. *Frugal*—I will be wise with my money and spend it
    only on things that are of necessity. (9)

25. *Reward*—I will reward others and myself when
    goals are achieved. (11, 13)

26. *Trust*—I will be trustworthy and trust others and in
    the Lord. (5, 9, 13, 20)

27. *Laugh*—I will laugh often and especially in intense
    situations to relieve the stress and help me
    realize that the world won't end if things do not
    turn out as planned. (9)

28. *Balance*—I will be balanced in my life and
    strengthen my weaknesses in becoming more
    complete. (4, 13, 18)

My Goals

- Spiritual goals
    1. I will work daily to be worthy of eternal life with
       my heavenly Father when I pass away.
    2. I will pray daily.
    3. I will read daily (scriptures/spiritual books).
    4. I will home teach monthly.
    5. I will teach 4–6 post discussions a month.
    6. I will pay my tithing monthly.
    7. I will write in my journal weekly.

8. I will analyze my spirituality daily to find out my strengths and weaknesses.

- Physical goals
  1. I will work out daily.
  2. I will eat healthy food daily.
  3. I will not smoke.
  4. I will not drink alcohol, coffee, or tea.
  5. I will play tennis or volleyball twice a week.
  6. I will eat 3–4 meals a day at the appropriate times and the right proportions.
  7. I will take my daily vitamins.
  8. I will sleep at least 7 hours a day.

- Familial goals
  1. I will contact each family member at least every other week.
  2. I will work daily to become a better listener and stop preaching so much whenever I speak with them.
  3. I will always drop anything I am doing for a family emergency starting today.
  4. I will tell my mother, father, brother, and sister that I love them any time I speak with them on the phone beginning today.
  5. I will be a good example for them at all times starting today.
  6. I will always keep my eyes open at all times for a possible spouse beginning today.
  7. I will pray for my family daily.
  8. I will have 3–4 children or the amount preferred by the Lord after marriage.
  9. I will travel to the Philippines with my family within the next two years.

- Societal goals
  1. I will be a good example daily.
  2. I will become a Market Maker within the next 1½ years.

3. I will go outside my comfort zone daily to meet new people and cheer up at least one person's day. (smile)
4. I will help Nedra with her Life Mapping weekly. (Thear)
5. I will assist Sandro in his short- and long-term goals twice a month. (mentor)
6. I will travel to Europe before the year 2000 and learn from the different cultures.
7. I will work to listen to others before placing judgment or opinion beginning today.
8. I will travel through Asia before the year 2002.

My Activity List

- Spiritual activities
    2a. and 3a. I will pray and read scriptures every day before I go to sleep.
    4a. I will home teach assigned members of church every first and third week of the month (once a month).
    7a. I will write in my journal every Sunday evening before sleep and jot down strengths and weaknesses during the week.
    8a. I will be grateful at all times of the day for the experiences and gifts which the Lord provides me.

- Physical activities
    1a. I will lift weights on Monday, Tuesday, Thursday, and Friday.
    1b. I will run on the treadmill on Monday, Wednesday, Thursday, and Saturday, unless fulfilled through tennis or volleyball.
    3a and 4a. I will not smoke, drink alcohol, or coffee or tea each day.
    5a. I will play tennis or volleyball on Wednesdays or Saturdays.

6a. I will eat 4 times a day.

6b. I will not eat dinner any later than 8 P.M.

7a. I will take my vitamins every morning.

8a. I will sleep 7 hours a day.

- Familial activities

  1a. I will contact at least 2 family members on Monday evening.

  2a. I will spend at least half of my conversation listening attentively to a family member.

  3a. I will drop anything at any time for a family emergency.

  6a. I will date at least once every two weeks.

  7a. I will pray for my family every evening before I go to sleep.

- Societal activities

  1a. I will try to follow Jesus' example constantly.

  2a. I will study 5 hours a week.

  2b. I will constantly ask Market Maker questions regarding options trading.

  3a. I will introduce myself to strangers whenever given the opportunity.

  4a. I will meet with Life Mapping families (Nedra/ Thurs. evening) or with Thear whenever needed.

  5a. I will meet with Sandro (mentee) every other week.

RICHARD'S 1997 SCHEDULE

Time	Monday	Tuesday	Wednesday	Thursday	Friday	Saturday	Sunday
4:30	Wake up	Wake up	Wake up	Wake up	Wake up	stretch/shower	stretch/shower
5:00	breakfast/grooming	breakfast/grooming	breakfast/grooming	breakfast/grooming	breakfast/grooming		
5:30	travel to work	travel to work	travel to work	travel to work	travel to work		
6:00	work	work	work	work	work		
9:00	work	work	work	work	work	wake up	wake up
9:30	work	work	work	work	work		breakfast/grooming
10:00	lunch	lunch	lunch	lunch	lunch		church
11:00	work	work	work	work	work	something active	church
1:00	work	work	work	work	work		home teaching
2:00	go home	go home	go home	go home	go home		
3:00	workout	workout	tennis	workout	workout		
4:00	cardio/sit-ups	sit-ups	tennis	cardio/sit-ups	sit-ups		
4:30	shopping		tennis				
5:00	study/read	study/read	study/read	study/read	study/read		
7:00					friends		call family
8:00	friends			call Nedra			review/plan
9:00	read	read	read	read			read
10:00	sleep	sleep	sleep	sleep			sleep
11:00	sleep	sleep	sleep	sleep	read	read	sleep

Nedra's Life Map

The Purpose of Life

To help others and thereby achieve everlasting life with
God in heaven.

The Purpose of My Life

My purpose is to successfully raise my children and to
care for the sick.

My Belief List

1. I believe that there is a God Almighty, Ruler of the
   Universe.
2. I believe God created heaven and earth.
3. I believe we were put here to make choices. (Good
   or bad)
4. I believe everyone was created equally.
5. I believe everyone has a God, let it be dog, statue
   or tree.
6. I believe we were put here to live and die.
7. I believe everyone has a right to life and not to take
   another.
8. I believe everyone has the right to voice their opinion.
9. I believe if you want something bad enough you
   will work hard to achieve that goal.
10. I believe the children are our future. (Teach them well.)
11. I believe I can stop smoking.
12. I believe with a little direction and guidance my
    son Nolan will get a good education.
13. I believe beauty is only skin deep. If you hurt us
    we will cry. Take off the skin and there is a
    person still underneath.
14. I believe Jesus Christ is the son of God.

15. I believe to have everlasting life you will have to live by God's word.

The Principle List

1. I will not kill. (7)
2. I will respect others' decisions and choices whether I believe in them or not. (As long as it hurts no one) (8)
3. I will treat people as I want to be treated. (4)
4. I will respect others regardless of their race or skin color. (13)
5. I will strive to make sure my child has a good education. (Teachers can't be their only tool.) (10, 12)
6. I will continue to work hard. (9)
7. I will strive for excellence, in all that I do in service to myself and others. (9)
8. I will succeed in choices I made at Thear for my future. (9)
9. I will stop smoking. With lots of hard work and support. (11)
10. I will live my life as a Christian. (15)

My Goals

- Spiritual goals
  1. To pray 3 times a day.
  2. To be baptized this year.
  3. To go to church monthly.

- Physical goals
  1. To gain weight this year.
  2. To stop smoking this year.

- Familial goals
  1. To create budget this month.
  2. Family bonding with children daily.
  3. Put son on schedule starting today.

- Societal goals
    1. To volunteer my time in the nursing field
        in August.
    2. Become an LVN within five years.
        (Licensed Vocational Nurse)

My Activity List

- Spiritual activities
    1a. Bring children together for praying time.
    1b. I will establish praying time.
    1c. On the way to work, at dinner time, bedtime.
    2a. To go to church.
    2b. To talk to pastors, reverends, ministers, etc.
    2c. To hear the word of God, and learn from what
        you have been taught.
    2d. To have that spiritual feeling in your heart.
    2e. To repent all sins.
    3a. To go to church . . . 10:00 Sunday School . . .
        11:00 Reg. Church Services
    3b. Get up.
    3c. Get cleaned up (shower, bath, brush teeth).
    3d. Have breakfast.
    3e. Get dressed.
    3f. Check children over.
    3g. Warm up car.
    3h. Off we go.

- Physical activities
    1a. Talk to dietician/nutritionist
    1b. Response.
    1c. Eat more frequently.
    1d. Small meals—6 times a day.
    1e. Take vitamins. One a day . . . Centrum.
    1f. Eat proteins, fish, chicken, eggs.
    1g. Take snacks along with you when going
        somewhere.

1h. Example: Cookies, wafers, graham crackers, lunch meat, jelly beans.
1i. Call in 2 weeks . . . I pound a week . . . June 30.
2a. Talk to pharmacist about how long to use the patch. (Reply 6–8 wks)
2b. Save money . . . $150.00 . . . June 30
2c. Buy patch and gum.
2d. Remove cigarettes, ashtrays, and lighters.
2e. Make up mind to stop.
2f. Use patch and gum.
2g. Successfully completed by August 25, 1997.
2h. Call Bill on anniversary. (Once a month)

- Familial activities
  1a. Work with Bill to create written budget.
  2a. Select date and time each week to have dinner together, pray.
  2b. Family council meetings.
  2c. This time is sacred, no phone calls, TV, nothing else to be scheduled.
  2d. Choose monthly date for other family members.
  3a. Decide on bedtime . . . 9:00–9:30.
  3b. Eat dinner.
  3c. Make sure homework is done.
  3d. Let Nolan pick out his school clothes for next day.
  3e. Take bath.
  3f. Pull covers back.
  3g. Say prayers.
  3h. Good Night.

- Societal activities
  1a. Volunteer at 1275 Crane.
  1b. Sometime after August 1.
  1c. Volunteer 4 times a month, 4 to 16 hours.
  2a. Information Session . . . May 6.

2b. Sign up for counseling 1 class . . . July 28,
    1997–August 14, 1997.
2c. Fall '97.
    i. Reading 161 . . . August 18, 1997–December
        23, 1997
    ii. English 105 . . . August 18, 1997–December
        20, 1997.
2d. Oct '97
    i. Make appt. to see counselor.
2e. Spring '98
    i. Reading 53
    ii. English 108a
2f. Fall '98
    i. Math 102
    ii. Biosc. 55—Anatomy Physiology
    iii. Ahool-CPR—Cardiopulmonary Resuscitation
2g. Spring '99
    i. AH 3—Medical Terminology
    ii. VN57—Introduction to Gerontology
    iii. Apply for Regular Program.
2h. Fall '99
    i. Psych-12—Human Growth and Development
    ii. NS40 or WS15—Diet in Health and Disease
    iii. Apply for Regular Program.
2i. Spring 2000
    i. Vn59 A—Beginning Pharmacology Part 1
    ii. Biosc. 5—Anatomy and Physiology
    iii. Apply for Regular Program.
2j. Fall 2000
    i. Semester A
        1. Medical/Surgical Clinical Lab
        2. Medical/Surgical Nursing Theory
        3. Communication and Behavior
        4. Nursing Process
        5. Beginning Pharmacology—Part 1

2k. Spring 2001
    i. Semester B
        1. Medical/Surgical Clinical Lab
        2. Medical/Surgical Nursing Theory
        3. Obstetrics
        4. Beginning Pharmacology Part 2
        5. Diet in Health and Disease
        6. Human Growth and Development
2l. Fall 2001
    i. Semester C
        1. Medical/Surgical Clinical Lab
        2. Medical/Surgical Nursing Theory
        3. Seminar in Issues and Trends
        4. Introduction to Child Health Care
        5. Introduction to Gerontology
2m. Receive Vocational Nurse License.

NEDRA'S 1997 SCHEDULE

TIME	MONDAY	TUESDAY	WEDNESDAY	THURSDAY	FRIDAY	SATURDAY	SUNDAY
4:30	get up	get up	get up	get up		get up	
5:00	get ready	get ready	get ready	get ready		get ready	
5:30	pray/go to work	pray/go to work	pray/go to work	pray/go to work		pray/go to work	
6:00	work	work	work	work	get up	work	get up
8:00	snack	snack	snack	snack	pray/eat	snack	pray/eat
9:00	work	work	work	work	Nolan to school	work	dress children
10:00	work	work	work	work	iron	work	church
11:00	snack	snack	snack	snack	wash	snack	church
1:00	snack	snack	snack	snack	wash dishes	snack	church
2:00	volunteer	go home	go home	volunteer	start dinner	volunteer	pray/eat
3:00	clean house	go to school	go to school		volunteer	clean house	iron
4:00	make dinner	reading 161	English 105	make dinner	homework	playtime	make dinner
5:00	pray/eat	reading 161	English 105	pray/eat	homework	play time	pray/eat
7:00	homework	reading 161	English 105	wash dishes	finish dinner	make dinner	clean house
8:00	homework	pray/eat	pray/eat	homework	pray/eat	pray/eat	playtime
8:30	homework	family time	family time	homework	family time	family time	children bath
9:00	pray/bedtime	pray/bedtime	pray/bedtime	pray/bedtime	pray/bedtime	pray/bedtime	pray/bedtime
9:30	relax	relax	relax	relax	relax	relax	relax
10:00	final chores	final chores	final chores	final chores	final chores	final chores	final chores

Ray's Life Map

The Purpose of Life

We are here to discover our purpose, to live it, and to share the process with others.

The Purpose of My Life

My purpose in life is to be a lifelong learner and to share my knowledge with others. It is a process of self-discovery as well as enlightenment.

My Belief List

1. I believe in a power greater than myself which I choose to call God.
2. I believe God dwells in all things and in all people.
3. I believe God loves me unconditionally.
4. I believe God keeps his promises and honors his commitments to me.
5. I believe in Alcoholics Anonymous.
6. I believe in total honesty with myself and others.
7. I believe I will succeed in my chosen career.
8. I believe it is my path to follow through in my choices, commitments, and responsibilities because God gave me the gifts of free will and the power of choice.
9. I believe it is God's will for me to love and believe in myself so that I may be of maximum service to God and his children.
10. I believe it is my responsibility to be truthful and loyal in all areas of my life—why?
11. I believe it is God's will for me to be happy, joyous, and free.

The Principle List

1. I will use God's will in my life and my actions to help myself and others. (9)
2. I will respect all people's beliefs even if they are different from mine providing that they cause no harm to others. (2)
3. I will be the very best father I can learn to be. (2, 3, 8, 10)
4. I will practice total honesty in all aspects of my life. (6, 10)
5. I will honor my commitments to myself first and to all others. (8, 9)
6. I will take initiative in my decision making toward being successful and improving the quality of my life and my family's life. (7, 8)
7. I will admonish myself to be loyal and true to the people and things I believe in. (4, 6, 10)
8. I will love my children Joshua and Sarah unconditionally. (1, 2, 3, 4, 8)

My Goals

- Societal goals
    1. I will obtain a Novel CNE certification level 4 within one year (based on finances and new budget).
    2. I will obtain an A.S. degree in data. communications from Foothill College within five years.
    3. I will spend four hours a month volunteering at Thear.
    4. I will have car insurance within six months.

- Physical goals
    1. I will develop a food plan with dietitian within six months.
    2. I will weigh 180 lbs. within two years.

3. I will exercise every other day to start when my Life Map is complete.
4. I will quit smoking within one year.

- Spiritual goals
    1. I will complete my first Life Map within the next three weeks and continue to update it once a month.
    2. I will read positive literature weekly.
    3. I will find a place to fellowship on a regular basis within six months.
    4. I will pray and meditate on a regular basis. (every other day)

- Family goals
    1. I will find a safe place to live by July first.
    2. I will use my daily planner every day and keep track of my time and expenses daily.
    3. I will have a budget within three weeks and review it on a bimonthly basis.
    4. I will have a reliable car within one year.
    5. I will determine a way to review my progress as a role model to my kids.
    6. I will determine a time on a daily basis for my kids to have my full attention.
    7. I will repay my outstanding debts within five years.

My Activity List

- Societal activities
    1a. In my new schedule I will incorporate the time needed to complete each of the nine segments for the CNE certification.
    1b. I will determine from Lanop if there is any financing that I can qualify for so that I can reach my goal sooner.

1c. Upon completion of a new budget I will need to determine how long it will take to save $6,365.

    i. My schedule and budget will also need to include the cost for baby-sitting and to find a quality person for watching my kids while I am working and going to school.

1d. Begin Lanop July 15, 1997.

1e. Complete Lanop June 8, 1998.

1f. Upon completion of this goal I will enter the work force within this industry hopefully at a salary range of $40,000 dollars a year and be better able to provide for my family.

1g. A long-range goal will be to work a number of years in this career and become self-employed as a consultant so that I may free up more time for my family and help others to learn what has been so freely given to me and my family.

2a. Upon completing my career goal I will return to school to obtain my A.S. degree.

3a. I have asked Bill Cohen how I can help Thear and was told until a new group starts this process I can do some computer work to help out. I will include this time in my completed schedule.

4a. Upon a completed budget I will determine the soonest I can buy insurance.

- Physical activities
    - 1a. I will set up a meeting with Jean Muller by October 1, 1997.
    - 2a. After completing a food plan I will have a better idea on how to accomplish this goal.

2b. In my meeting with a dietitian I will be
    asking for advice on how to accomplish
    this goal.

3a. I will walk every other day for twenty minutes,
    to be included in my schedule.

3b. This goal will directly aid in accomplishing goal
    No. 2.

4a. I will outline a plan of actions to quit smoking
    by February 1, 1998.

- Spiritual activities
    1a. I will continue to keep all appointments with
        Thear and Bill Cohen.
    1b. I will place a time in my completed schedule for
        regular review of my Life Map.
    2a. I will place a time in my schedule for doing
        this activity.
    2b. I will use this time slot to also determine a
        reading list and acquire the books.
    3a. I will include time for this activity in my
        schedule.
    3b. I will attend different churches to find one that
        my family and I can be comfortable at.
    4a. I will include time for this activity in my
        schedule.

- Family activities
    1a. I will network to everyone I know to find a
        place.
    1b. I will keep all appointments with my contacts.
    1c. In my new budget I will determine how I
        will manage the money to accomplish this
        goal.
    2a. In my schedule I will have a time to review my
        daily planner.
    3a. I will set up an appointment with Bill Cohen or
        Nat Holmes to review my finances.

4a. After completing a budget I will set so much
money aside to accomplish this goal.

5a. In reviewing my Map monthly I will gain insight
on my activities as a role model.

6a. Upon a completed Life Map in my schedule
there will be a time slot for this goal.

6b. Upon further review of my Map, I will
determine what activities to insert into
this time slot.

7a. Within my completed budget I will allow for this
repayment.

RAY'S 1997 SCHEDULE WITH KIDS

TIME	MONDAY	TUESDAY	WEDNESDAY	THURSDAY	FRIDAY	SATURDAY	SUNDAY
5:30	shower/plan	shower/plan	shower/plan	shower/plan	shower/plan	shower/plan	
6:00	meditate	meditate	meditate	meditate	meditate	meditate	
6:30	kids to school	kids to school	kids to school	kids to school	kids to school	kids to sitter	shower/plan
7:00	work	work	work	work	work	market	leave for mtg
7:30	work	work	work	work	work	grocery	AA meeting
9:30	work	work	work	work	work	fun	leave for Nat's
10:00	lunch	lunch	lunch	lunch	lunch	lunch	
11:30	work	work	work	work	work	fun	leave to get kids
12:00	work	work	work	work	work	fun	p/u kids
12:30	eat/network	eat/network	eat/network	eat/network	eat/network	eat/network	lunch
1:00	work	work	work	work	work	fun	laundry/naps
5:00	p/u kids	p/u kids	p/u kids	p/u kids	p/u kids	p/u kids	
6:00	dinner	dinner	dinner	dinner	dinner	dinner	dinner
7:00	kids time	kids time	kids time	kids time	shopping	kids time	kids
8:30	kids bed	kids bed	kids bed	kids bed	kids bed	kids bed	kids bed
9:30	study	study	study	study	study		study
11:00	plan/pray	plan/pray	plan/pray	plan/pray	sarah bed	sarah bed	budget/map
11:30	sleep	sleep	sleep	sleep	plan/pray	plan/pray	sleep
12:00	sleep	sleep	sleep	sleep	sleep	sleep	sleep

RAY'S 1997 SCHEDULE WITHOUT KIDS

TIME	MONDAY	TUESDAY	WEDNESDAY	THURSDAY	FRIDAY	SATURDAY	SUNDAY
5:30	shower/plan	shower/plan	shower/plan	shower/plan	shower/plan	shower/plan	
6:00	meditate	meditate	meditate	meditate	meditate	meditate	
6:30	breakfast/work	breakfast/work	breakfast/work	breakfast/work	breakfast/work		shower/plan
7:00	work	work	work	work	work		breakfast
7:30	work	work	work	work	work		Lanop
9:30	work	work	work	work	work	Lanop	Lanop
10:00	lunch	lunch	lunch	lunch	lunch	Lanop	Lanop
11:30	work	work	work	work	work	Lanop	Lanop
12:00	work	work	work	work	work	Lanop	Lanop
12:30	eat/network	eat/network	eat/network	eat/network	eat/network	Lanop	Lanop
1:00	work	work	work	work	work	Lanop	Lanop
5:00						Lanop	
6:00	Lanop	Lanop	Lanop	Lanop	Lanop	dinner	dinner
7:00	Lanop	Lanop	Lanop	Lanop	Lanop		walk
8:30	Lanop	Lanop	Lanop	Lanop	Lanop		
9:30		walk		walk			
11:00	plan/pray	plan/pray	plan/pray	plan/pray	sarah bed		plan/pray
11:30	sleep	sleep	sleep	sleep	plan/pray	plan/pray	sleep
12:00	sleep	sleep	sleep	sleep	sleep	sleep	sleep

Bernadette's Life Map

The Purpose of Life

The purpose of one's life is to realize and fulfill the purpose(s) of one's own unique existence, therefore achieving true, pure happiness.

The Purpose of My Life

The purpose of my life is to realize and fulfill my own purpose(s), determined by God, and therefore achieve true and pure happiness.

My Belief List

1. I believe that there is a God, a greater being than all life, who has a plan for all life, and is more complex than we can yet understand.
2. I believe we experience manifestations of God every day.
3. I believe that all life is connected.
4. I believe life is sacred.
5. I believe that life and its uniqueness and individuality should be respected.
6. I believe in the fundamental goodness of all life I know of at this time.
7. I believe that every person desires to be wholly his/herself who they were meant by God to be, or fully human; this is to say that they desire to be true to themselves and complete.
8. I believe every person needs to be loved—and to know it.
9. I believe all of us are capable of loving everyone else.

10. I believe that privileges and responsibility go hand in hand.
11. I believe that inflexibility and ignorance are at the core of all catastrophes.
12. I believe that, at any time, these beliefs may—and possibly should—change.

The Principle List

1. I will keep an open mind (11)
2. I will respect others, their existence, and their pursuit of happiness and full humanity. (7)
3. I will find something to love about every person I come in contact with. (8, 9)
4. I will pray or commune with God every day. (2, 3)
5. I will accept responsibility for my actions. (10)

My Goals

- Spiritual goals
  1. I will view reading with more acceptance and joy starting today.

- Familial goals
  1. I will be a good mother.

- Physical goals
  1. I will take a self-defense class this year.

- Societal goals
  1. I will do my homework more faithfully.

My Activity List

- Spiritual activities
  1a. I will complete my reading homework every night.

1b. I will take a break between each reading assignment.

1c. I will carry a book to read with me at all times.

1d. I will read for three hours or more each week this summer.

1e. I will maintain a bookmark in the place where I start each reading session.

1f. I will challenge myself to read faster and longer each session, if appropriate.

- Familial activities

    1a. I will practice having patience with my family, brothers, and friends.

    1b. To practice parenting I will help with chores more often; offer to help whenever I truly can.

    1c. I will baby-sit conscientiously.

    1d. I will initiate discussions and ask for advice from my parents and others' parents.

    1e. I will discuss parenting with my potential husband to make sure we agree.

    1f. I will make sure that housing and income are suitable before I have children.

    1g. I will read books to my children.

    1h. I will make sure I spend enough time with my children.

    1i. I will be active; encouraging questioning, development, security, happiness, joy, wonderment, etc.

- Physical activities

    1a. I will look for classes at community colleges and centers.

    1b. I will compare times, prices, and eligibility.

    1c. I will sign up.

    1d. I will not miss a class or practice.

- Societal activities
  - 1a. I will set aside two or more hours daily in my schedule for homework.
  - 1b. I will write down, in my notebook, each homework assignment when it is announced.
  - 1c. I will make sure that my work area is clean and comfortable.
  - 1d. I will take breaks when needed.
  - 1e. I won't waste time or take unreasonably long breaks during study time.
  - 1f. I will reassess priorities if my homework exceeds the time I have allotted.

BERNADETTE'S 1997 SCHEDULE

Time	Monday	Tuesday	Wednesday	Thursday	Friday	Saturday	Sunday
5:30		up/study	up/study				
6:00	up/shower/ dress	up/shower/ dress	up/shower/ dress	up/shower/ dress	up/shower/ dress		
7:00	breakfast	breakfast	breakfast	breakfast	breakfast		
7:30	go to school	go to school	go to school	go to school	go to school		
8:00	school	school	school	school	school		
10:00	school	school	school	school	school	up	up
11:00	school	school	school	school	school	breakfast/ shower	breakfast/ shower
12:30	lunch	lunch	lunch	lunch	lunch	errands/free time	study
2:00	school	school	school	school	school	lunch	lunch
3:00	SAT class/ work	VB game/work	SAT class/ work	workout/work	VB game/work	workout	study
4:00						work	workout
5:00		dinner		dinner			dinner
6:00	history class	history class	history class	history class	go out	dinner	study
7:00						go out	
8:00	dinner	study	dinner	study			
9:00	study		study				free time
10:00	study/plan	study/plan	study/plan	study/plan			sleep
11:00	sleep	sleep	sleep	sleep			
12:00					sleep	sleep	

Nathalie's Life Map

The Purpose of Life

The defining of the person we are to be and the becoming of that person.

The Purpose of My Life

The purpose of my life is to define who I would like to be and strive to be that person no matter what. To become that person I need to understand that I will make mistakes. However, I cannot dwell on the mistakes but rather I need to learn from them. Also I cannot make excuses for myself but rather must have confidence that I can achieve if I work hard enough.

My Belief List

1. I believe in a greater power than myself.
2. I believe that honesty is necessary to have a genuine relationship.
3. I believe all people are valuable because of their individuality, which is fundamental to human nature, and thus deserve respect.
4. I believe in love.
5. I believe all people possess the capacity to do good.
6. I believe all people have the right to speak their mind.
7. I believe in personal space.
8. I believe that all people are interconnected and therefore must make decisions regarding others. "No man/woman is an island" no matter how hard he/she tries.
9. I believe personal pain is never an excuse to cause others pain.

The Principle List

1. I will be honest in order to keep my relationships real. (2)
2. I will value and respect others because of their basic individuality. (3)
3. I will acknowledge all people's capacity to do good and try to help them fill that capacity. (5)
4. I will respect others' personal space. (7)
5. I will do my best to love all people. (4)
6. I will make my decisions for myself but I will not forget that what I do affects everyone else. (8)
7. I will never cause anyone else pain no matter how horrible I feel myself. (9)

My Goals

- Spiritual goals
    1. Define my relationship with the power greater than myself and explore the possibilities of that relationship beginning today.

- Familial goals
    1. Learn to appreciate and respect both my father and my stepfather this year.

- Societal goals
    1. Write a real magazine for real women within ten years.

- Physical goals
    1. Learn to eat correctly and healthily beginning next month.

My Activity List

- Spiritual activities
    1a. Check out a book a month on a different religion each time.

    1b. Write a page a week in my journal about how I define the power greater than myself.

    1c. Be completely open to other forms of thought.

    1d. Learn to meditate in order to free my mind to other thoughts.

    1e. Talk to other people about what they think.

    1f. Define who that power is and what the manifestations of "it" are.

    1g. Learn how to appreciate the manifestations of that power.

    1h. Appreciate small moments.

- Familial activities

    1a. Discipline myself to listen when they speak.

    1b. Acknowledge that they are human and do possess both bad and good qualities instead of making them into inhuman monsters.

    1c. Make myself spend time with each of them at least once a month for an hour.

- Societal activities

    1a. Read magazines and evaluate, record opinions.

    1b. Get a job in a magazine/newspaper.

    1c. Take classes in journalism, publishing, editing.

    1d. Talk to father, ask for tour of a magazine.

    1e. Create title, sections for individual subjects.

    1f. Decide style, contents.

    1g. Research amount of support for topic.

    1h. Decide what target audience is.

    1i. Look for ads.

    1j. Finalize plans, set deadlines.

    1k. Set up regular "check-ins" to make sure we believe in what we are writing and stay true to ideals.

    1l. Create a budget, iron out little specifics.

    1m. Make money through ads, jobs.

    1n. Hire a publisher, editor.

    1o. Get supplies and equipment.

    1p. Get a legal consultant, make sure all legal needs
        are met.

    1q. Advertise.

    1r. Deal with the problems.

    1s. Write a mission statement.

    1t. Outlines for magazine evolution; determine
        what's okay.

- Physical activities
  - 1a. Make an appointment at the nutritionist.
  - 1b. Clean out the refrigerator and cupboards of all unwanted food.
  - 1c. Reward myself for each week done healthily.
  - 1d. Read a book a month on how to eat healthily.
  - 1e. Attend OA meetings.
  - 1f. Take healthful cooking classes, at least 3 a year.

NATHALIE'S 1997 SCHEDULE

TIME	MONDAY	TUESDAY	WEDNESDAY	THURSDAY	FRIDAY	SATURDAY	SUNDAY
6:00	run/move	run/move	run/move	run/move	run/move		
6:30	bagels	run/move	bagels	run/move	bagels		
7:00	get ready	get ready	get ready	get ready	get ready		
7:30	garden	garden	garden	garden	garden		get ready
8:00	school	school	school	school	school		work
11:30						get ready/work	
1:30						work	lunch
2:00							friends
3:00	people	people	people	people	people		
4:00		work	beach	work	work	homework	
4:30	paint/write				paint/write		
5:00	talk/ homework				friends	garden	garden
6:00	dinner		dinner		dinner	run/move	run/move
6:30	homework		homework		friends	dinner	dinner
7:00	read/ homework	read/ homework	read/ homework	read/ homework		friends	talk
8:00		sleep		sleep			read
9:00	sleep		sleep				homework
10:00							sleep

Bill's Life Map
(Updated July 1997)

The Purpose of Life

We are here to develop into the kind of beings in whose company God would want to spend eternity.

The Purpose of My Life

My purpose is to understand life and relationships, live it in alignment with that understanding, and finally, to teach others the process.

My Belief List

1. I believe only God could create a world with the potential for perfection that exists today.
2. I believe there is a God.
3. I believe God created a blueprint for evolution because He wanted us to develop into His family.
4. I believe God placed a blueprint for life within each of us, so that each of us could do our part in the evolutionary process.
5. I believe each of us has a unique blueprint, since each of us plays a different role in the evolutionary process.
6. I believe we are all equal in God's eyes, we are all God's children.
7. I believe God wants us to be treated equally, as any parent who truly loves their children would.
8. I believe life is eternal and is meant to be shared with God.
9. I believe God will unite with us when we understand and follow our unique blueprint.

10. I believe everyone has the ability to reach their individual level of perfection.
11. I believe only the Son of God could have lived a perfect life as an example for us all.
12. I believe Jesus is the Son of God.

My Principle List

1. I will work to develop the following virtues into habits: I will

a. be honest	g. be helpful
b. be cooperative	h. be supportive
c. be reliable	i. be trustworthy
d. be loyal	j. be respectful
e. be humble	k. be tranquil
f. be patient	l. be confident

These principles are supported by belief numbers 2, 3, 4, 5, 7, 9, 10.
2. I will be industrious, frugal, alert, physically fit, will respect order and work toward the development of my special skills. (1, 3, 4, 5, 8, 9, 10)

My Goals List

- Spiritual goals
    1. Communicate daily with God.
    2. Read daily.
    3. Attend church weekly.
    4. Learn to meditate this year.

- Familial goals
    1. Have some fun weekly.
    2. Have daily contact.

- Societal goals
    1. Keep active daily in State Farm career.

2. Give back to the community weekly.
3. Keep playing games weekly.
4. Write a new book every three years.

- Physical goals
    1. Have a balanced nutritional program starting today.
    2. Stay fit through daily exercise.
    3. Integrate fun into exercises.
    4. Maintain weight at 170–180.

My Activity List

- Spiritual activities
    1a. Set aside 30 minutes every morning to pray and listen.
    2a. Prioritize book list every Sunday night. (Weekly list)
    2b. Read every night before bed.
    3a. Go to church every Sunday after basketball.
    4a. Research available classes—between appointments next week at work.
    4b. Take another meditation class.
    4c. Evaluate progress and repeat process if necessary.

- Familial activities
    1a. Set time to schedule some kind of game weekly. (Weekly list)
    2a. Go over schedule with Gail daily.
    2b. Have a Family Council meeting weekly/monthly.
    2c. Plan weekly date night with Gail. (Weekly list)
    2d. Call Dad, Bob, or Diane weekly. (Weekly list)
    2e. Weekly ask others if I can be of help. (Weekly list)

- Societal activities

  1a. Develop regular work schedule.

  1b. Work 37-hour schedule at my office—5, 7, 7, 8, 5, 5.

  2a. Volunteer 6 hours weekly to Thear. (Weekly list)

  2b. Volunteer 2 hours weekly to Kiwanis.

  3a. Set time to schedule some kind of game with friend, every Monday, to schedule play time. (Weekly list)

  4a. Schedule time to work on book daily.

  4b. Decide on topic for next book (September). (Weekly list)

  4c. Research (October–December). (Weekly list)

  4d. Outline (January–April). (Weekly list)

  4e. Draft (May–August). (Weekly list)

  4f. Produce final product (September–December). (Weekly list)

Physical activities

  1a. Take vitamins daily.

  1b. Eat a balanced diet—plan with Gail. (Weekly list)

  2a. Walk daily with Gail.

  3a. Play some golf, tennis, and basketball—call friend, every Monday, to schedule game. (Weekly list)

  4a. Weigh myself daily and adjust food consumption.

BILL'S 1997 SCHEDULE

Time	Monday	Tuesday	Wednesday	Thursday	Friday	Saturday	Sunday
6:00	Pray/Meditate	Pray/Meditate	Pray/Meditate	Pray/Meditate	Pray/Meditate	Sleep	Sleep
6:30	Feed Kids/Eat	Feed Kids/Eat	Feed Kids/Eat	Feed Kids/Eat	Feed Kids/Eat	"	"
7:00	Plan/Walk	Plan/Walk	Plan/Walk	Plan/Walk	Plan/Walk	Pray/Meditate	Pray/Meditate
7:30	Get Ready	Get Ready	Get Ready	Get Ready	Get Ready	Plan/Walk	Plan/Walk
8:00	Read/Write	Read/Write	Read/Write	Read/Write	Read/Write	Eat	Eat
8:30	"	"	"	"	Thear		Basketball
9:00	Office	"	"	Appointment	"	Office	"
9:30	"	"	"	"	Office	Appointment	"
10:00	"	Appointment	Inspect/Play	Office	Appointment	"	Church
10:30	"	"	"	Appointment	"	Office	"
11:00	"	Office	"	"	Office	Appointment	Family Council
11:30	"	Kiwanis	"	Office	"	"	"
12:00	Eat	"	Eat	Eat	Eat	Eat	Eat
1:00	Office	"	Inspect/Play	Office	Office	Organize Off/Home	
1:30	Thear	"	"	"	"	"	
2:00	"	Appointment	"	Appointment	Appointment	Thear	
2:30	Office	"	"	"	"	"	
3:00	"	Office	"	Thear	Office	"	
3:30	"	"	"	"	"	"	
4:00	"	Appointment	"	Read/Write	Appointment	"	
4:30	"	"	"	"	"	"	
5:00	"	Office	"	"			
5:30	Eat	"	Eat	Eat	Eat	Eat	Eat
6:00		Appointment			Do Dishes	Fun	
6:30	Read/Write	"			Date Night	"	
7:00	"	Eat			"	"	
7:30	"		Meditation Class		"	"	
8:00	"		"		"	"	Call Family
8:30	"			Order Groceries	"	"	Update Book List
9:00	"	Read/Write	Read/Write	Pay Bills	"	"	Pay Bills
9:30	"	"	"	Read/Write	"	"	Review Week
10:00	Sleep	Sleep	Sleep	Sleep	"	"	Sleep
10:30	"	"	"	"	"	"	"
11:00	"	"	"	"	Sleep	Sleep	"
11:30	"	"	"	"	"	"	"
12:00	"	"	"	"	"	"	"

Appendix B

Sample Budgets

	$2,000	$3,000	$5,000	$8,000	$15,000	$20,000	$25,000
GROSS MONTHLY INCOMES	$2,000	$3,000	$5,000	$8,000	$15,000	$20,000	$25,000
TAXES	400	600	900	1,200	2,250	3,0000	3,750
NET MONTHLY INCOMES	$1,600	$2,400	$4,100	$6,800	$12,750	$17,000	$21,250
RETIREMENT—10%	160	240	410	680	1,275	1,700	2,125
CHARITY—10%	160	240	410	680	1,275	1,700	2,125
DEBT/RESERVE/LONG-TERM—10%	160	240	410	680	1,275	1,700	2,125
HOUSING—35%	560	840	1,435	2,380	4,462	5,950	8,750
FOOD—11%	250	375	451	748	1,402	1,870	2,338
LEISURE—8%	50	100	328	544	1,020	1,360	1,700
HEALTH CARE—5%	90	125	205	340	638	850	1,250
UTILITIES—5%	67	90	205	340	638	850	1,250
TRANSPORTATION—4%	70	100	164	272	510	680	850
CLOTHING—2%	33	50	82	136	255	340	425

Notes

Chapter 1: The Gathering

1. Quoted in William J. Bennett, *The Book of Virtues* (New York: Simon & Schuster, 1993), pp. 812–814.
2. Quoted in Tod Barnhart, *The Five Rituals of Wealth* (New York: HarperCollins, 1995) p. 58.

Chapter 3: Beliefs

1. Andy Andrews, *Storms of Perfection* (Nashville: Lightning Crown Publishers, 1992), p. 67.
2. C. S. Lewis, *The Magician's Nephew* (New York: Macmillan, 1955, p. 41.
3. Quoted in Marc Allen, *As You Think* (San Rafael, Calif.: Whatever Publishing, 1987), pp. 3–4.
4. John D. Rockefeller, Jr.

Chapter 4: Principles

1. H. Jackson Brown, Jr., *Life's Little Instruction Book* (Nashville: Rutledge Hill Press, 1991).
2. Tom Landry with Greg Lewis, *Tom Landry: An Autobiography* (New York: HarperCollins, 1991).
3. Tod Barnhart, *The Five Rituals of Wealth* (New York: HarperCollins, 1995), pp. 26–27.
4. Benjamin Franklin, *Benjamin Franklin. The Autobiography and Other Writings* (New York: Signet Classics, 1961), pp. 95, 103.
5. Edgar A. Guest, *Favorite Verse of Edgar A. Guest* (New York: Permabooks, 1950), p. 12.
6. Tom Hanks, "The Smartest Advice," *Family Circle,* November 1996, p. 8.
7. Michael Levine, *Lessons at the Halfway Point: Wisdom for Midlife* (Berkeley, Calif.: Celestial Arts, 1995).
8. Rabbi Marc Gellman, and Msgr. Thomas Hartman, *How Do You Spell God?* (New York: Morrow, 1995).
9. General H. Norman Schwarzkopf, "Quotable Quotes," *Reader's Digest.*

Chapter 5: Goals

1. Tod Barnhart, *The Five Rituals of Wealth* (New York: HarperCollins, 1995) p. 53.
2. James Allen, *As a Man Thinketh* (New York: Thomas Y. Crowell Company, 1981), p. 30.
3. Janine Buchanan, "Developing Your Business Plan," 1996, p. 10.
4. Cited in Stephen R. Covey, *The 7 Habits of Highly Effective People,* (New York: Simon & Schuster, 1989), pp. 278–279.
5. Michael Levine, *Lessons at the Halfway Point: Wisdom for Midlife* (Berkeley, Calif.: Celestial Arts, 1995).
6. H. Jackson Brown, Jr., *Life's Little Instruction Book* (Nashville: Rutledge Hill Press, 1991).
7. Dotson Rader, "Success? What About Happiness?" *Parade,* March 9, 1997, pp. 4–6.

Chapter 6: Activities

1. Hyrum W. Smith, *The 10 Natural Laws of Successful Time and Life Management* (New York: Warner Books, 1994), p. 190.
2. Quoted in Tod Barnhart, *The Five Rituals of Wealth* (New York: HarperCollins, 1995), p. 27.
3. Quoted in Andy Andrews, *Storms of Perfection* (Nashville: Lightning Crown Publishers, 1992), p. 107.
4. John Wooden, *They Call Me Coach* (Waco, Texas: Word, Inc., 1985), p. 105.
5. Quoted in ibid.
6. Admiral Bidcoff.
7. Quoted in Andrews, *Storms of Perfection*, p. 43.

Chapter 8: How To

1. Andrea Gemmet, "Role Model," *The Country Almanac*, March 5, 1997, pp. 16–17.
2. Alexandra Stoddard, *Living a Beautiful Life* (New York: Avon, 1986), p. 155.
3. James Michener, "Quotable Quotes," *Reader's Digest*.
4. John Wooden, *San Francisco Chronicle*.
5. Edgar A. Guest, *Favorite Verse of Edgar A. Guest* (New York: Permabooks, 1950), pp. 71–72.

Suggested Reading

Ahlers, Julia, Barbara Allaire, and Carl Koch. *Growing in Christian Morality*. Winona, Minn.: Saint Mary's Press, 1996.

Allen, James. *As a Man Thinketh*. New York: Thomas Y. Cromwell Company, 1981.

Allen, Marc. *As You Think*. San Rafael, Calif.: Whatever Publishing, Inc., 1987.

Barnhart, Tod. *The Five Rituals of Wealth: Proven Strategies for Turning the Little You Have into More Than Enough*. New York: HarperCollins, 1995.

Bennett, William J. *The Book of Virtues*. New York: Simon & Schuster, 1993.

Brown, H. Jackson, Jr. *Life's Little Instruction Book*. Nashville: Rutledge Hill Press, 1991.

Brown, Les. *Live Your Dreams*. New York: Morrow, 1992.

Covey, Stephen R. *The 7 Habits of Highly Effective People*. New York: Simon & Schuster, 1989.

Cowan, James. *A Mapmaker's Dream: The Meditations of Fra Mauro, Cartographer to the Court of Venice*. Boston: Shambhala Publications, 1996.

Franklin, Benjamin. *The Autobiography and Other Writings*. New York: Signet Classic, 1961.

Fritz, Robert. *The Path of Least Resistance: Learning to Become a Creative Force in Your Own Life*. New York: Ballantine, 1989.

Gellman, Rabbi Marc, and Msgr. Thomas Hartman. *How Do You Spell God?* New York: Morrow, 1995.

Guest, Edgar A. *Favorite Verse of Edgar A. Guest*. New York: Permabooks, 1950.

Hobbs, Charles R. *Time Power*. New York: Harper and Row, 1987.

The Holy Bible. Nashville: Regency Publishing House, 1976.

Jones, Laurie Beth. *Jesus CEO: Using Ancient Wisdom for Visionary Leadership*. New York: Hyperion, 1992.

Kushner, Harold. *When All You Ever Wanted Isn't Enough*. New York: Simon & Schuster, 1986.

Landry, Tom, with Gregg Lewis. *Tom Landry: An Autobiography*. New York: Walker & Company, 1991.

Levine, Michael. *Lessons at the Halfway Point: Wisdom for Midlife*. Berkeley: Celestial Arts, 1995.

Lewis, C. S. *The Magician's Nephew*. New York: Macmillan Publishing Company, 1955.

———. *Mere Christianity*. Westwood, N.J.: Barbour and Company, 1952.

Mandino, Og. *The Greatest Salesman in the World*. New York: Bantam Books, 1974.

Myers, David G. *The Pursuit of Happiness: Who Is Happy and Why*. New York: Morrow, 1992.

Pritikin, Robert. *The New Pritikin Program: The Easy and Delicious Way to Shed Fat, Lower Your Cholesterol, and Stay Fit*. New York: Simon & Schuster, 1990.

St. James, Elaine. *Living the Simple Life: A Guide to Scaling Down and Enjoying More*. New York: Hyperion, 1996.

Schlessinger, Dr. Laura. *How Could You Do That?! The Abdication of Character, Courage, and Conscience*. New York: HarperCollins, 1996.

Smith, Hyrum W. *The 10 Natural Laws of Successful Time and Life Management*. New York: Warner Books, 1994.

Stoddard, Alexandra. *Living a Beautiful Life*. New York: Avon, 1986.

Thoreau, Henry David. *Walden and Other Writings*. New York: The Modern Library, 1992.

Urban, Hal. *Life's Greatest Lessons or 20 Things I Want My Kid to Know*. Redwood City, Calif.: Great Lessons Press, 1992.

Wooden, John. *They Call Me Coach*. Waco, Texas: Word, Inc., 1985.

About the Author

To RECEIVE ADDITIONAL INFORMATION about Bill Cohen or Life Mapping, you can write to him at the following address:

Bill Cohen
325M Sharon Park Drive, #606
Menlo Park, CA 94025
650-323-8233

Please indicate your areas of interest:

- Life Mapping workshops and seminars.
- Life Mapping workbook
- Personal coaching in the Life Mapping process
- Thear International, a nonprofit organization dedicated to helping families escape poverty without government assistance
- Specially designed lectures or workshops based on Life Mapping
- Future books, audiotapes, and videotapes

Please make sure you clearly print your name, address, and fax number.